THIS IS
LOVE

Nina,
God has richly blessed you.
1 Thess 5:18
2 Cor 9:8
Jer 33:3

THIS IS
LOVE

New Discoveries into the Grace of God

SCOTT JOHNSON

TATE PUBLISHING
AND ENTERPRISES, LLC

Published by Tate Publishing & Enterprises, LLC
127 E. Trade Center Terrace | Mustang, Oklahoma 73064 USA
1.888.361.9473 | www.tatepublishing.com

Tate Publishing is committed to excellence in the publishing industry. The company reflects the philosophy established by the founders, based on Psalm 68:11,
"The Lord gave the word and great was the company of those who published it."

Book design copyright © 2013 by Tate Publishing, LLC. All rights reserved.
Cover design by Rtor Maghuyop
Interior design by Jomel Pepito

Published in the United States of America

ISBN: 978-1-62854-463-3
Religion / General
13.09.09

Bible Translations Used

In this is love: not that we loved God, but that He loved us and sent His Son to be the propitiation (the atoning sacrifice) for our sins.

1 John 4:10 (AMP)

For the grace of God (His unmerited favor and blessing) has come forward (appeared) for the deliverance from sin and the eternal salvation for all mankind.

Titus 2:11 (AMP)

Dedication

To my wife Rachel, the best example of
God's goodness and grace in my life

CONTENTS

PREFACE

Reasons to study and understand the truth about God's grace:

1. God tells us to grow in grace.

    > You therefore, beloved, knowing this beforehand, be on your guard so that you are not carried away by the error of unprincipled men and fall from your own steadfastness, but grow in the grace and knowledge of our Lord and Savior Jesus Christ. To Him be the glory, both now and to the day of eternity. Amen.
    >
    > 2 Peter 3:17–18 (NASB)

2. God tells us to be strengthened by grace.

    > Do not be carried away by varied and strange teachings; for it is good for the heart to be strengthened by grace, not by foods, through which those who were so occupied were not benefited.
    >
    > Hebrews 13:9 (NASB)

3. God tells us to teach the truth about grace.

> Those heretical teachers go to great lengths to flatter you, but their motives are rotten. They want to shut you out of the free world of God's grace so that you will always depend on them for approval and directions, making them feel important.

Galatians 4:17–18 (MSG)

4. Grace is meant for all people.

> For the grace of God has appeared, bringing salvation to all men

Titus 2:11 (NASB)

5. God's grace leads people to repentance.

> Or are you so blind as to trifle with and presume upon and despise and underestimate the wealth of His kindness and forbearance and long-suffering patience? Are you unmindful or actually ignorant of the fact that God's kindness is intended to lead you to repent (to change your mind and inner man to accept God's will)?

Romans 2:4 (AMP)

6. We need God's grace in order to serve God.

> Wherefore, a kingdom that cannot be shaken receiving, may we have grace, through which we

may serve God well-pleasingly, with reverence and religious fear;

Hebrews 12:28 (YLT)

7. The grace of God instructs (trains) us in godliness

> For the grace of God has appeared, bringing salvation to all men, instructing us to deny ungodliness and worldly desires, and to live sensibly, righteously and godly in the present age.

Titus 2:11–12 (NASB)

My hope is to keep my comments and writings in this book to a minimum and showcase the Word of God to let the truth in the Word speak to you. Nobody has a monopoly on truth. It's not about your or my opinion, but the truth in his Word. I pray that God will reveal his love to you in new ways through new revelation from his word.

And more importantly, I hope you start looking at God's Word and your relationship with him more and more through the understanding of the richness of his grace. The fruits of that include a clear conscience and freedom from condemnation, guilt, and shame. These are critical for you to lead a victorious life in Christ.

Paul explained the importance of the true Gospel of Grace very clearly by repeating a curse to anyone not teaching this true Gospel of Grace. Wow! Doesn't this mean that we need to know what he was talking about so that we are not accursed?

> I am amazed that you are so quickly deserting Him who called you by the grace of Christ, for a different gospel; which is really not another; only there are some who are disturbing you and want to distort the gospel of Christ. But even if we, or an angel from heaven, should preach to you a gospel contrary to what we have preached to you, he is to be accursed! As we have said before, so I say again now, if any man is preaching to you a gospel contrary to what you received, he is to be accursed! For am I now seeking the favor of men, or of God? Or am I striving to please men? If I were still trying to please men, I would not be a bond-servant of Christ.
>
> Galatians 1:6–10 (NASB)

The Word also tells us in more than one place that we should not be caught up in religious teachings of churches and traditions of men.

> Neglecting the commandment of God, you hold to the tradition of men. He was also saying to them, "You are experts at setting aside the commandment of God in order to keep your tradition"
>
> Mark 7:8–9 (NASB)

> See to it that no one takes you captive through philosophy and empty deception, according to the tradition of men, according to the elementary

principles of the world, rather than according to Christ.

Colossians 2:8 (NASB)

Do not be conformed to this world (this age), fashioned after and adapted to its external, superficial customs, but be transformed (changed) by the entire renewal of your mind by its new ideals and its new attitude, so that you may prove for yourselves what is the good and acceptable and perfect will of God, even the thing which is good and acceptable and perfect in His sight for you.

Romans 12:2 (AMP)

Thus you are nullifying and making void and of no effect the authority of the Word of God through your tradition, which you in turn hand on. And many things of this kind you are doing.

Mark 7:13 (AMP)

Finally, I want to express the same sentiment when Paul said it best in Galatians 1:10 above, for am I now seeking the favor of men, or of God? Or am I striving to please men? If I were still trying to please men, I would not be a bond-servant of Christ.

Thanks go out to the following ministers/ministries that played an important role in my life at some point; some to this day. Some are referenced in this book.

They are Andrew Wommack, Ken Copeland, Joyce Meyer, Jerry Savelle, Paula White

Creflo Dollar, Pastor Frankie Mazzapica, and Pastor Randy Harvey.

Additionally, special thanks go to Pastor Joseph Prince, whose ministry was the key inspiration for my writing this book.

My Year of Jubilee

Why did it take me 50 years to find peace and freedom?—My own personal testimony of God's Grace.

In the summer of 2006, I had just celebrated my fiftieth birthday. My personal life (and marriage) was in a mess. I went to the Ken Copeland Convention in Anaheim, California and cried out to God. I cried out and asked God why my marriage was falling apart, and thusly repeating a continuing cycle of failure.

In his goodness and grace, he spoke to my heart and said that my problem was that even though I had made Jesus my Saviour when I was seventeen years old, I never made him, Lord of my life. Instead, I was lord of my own life and lived a selfish life full of self-indulgence.

I suffered with one of those *secret sins*, as many in church often call them. It is not like the sins we commit often in public by being unkind in words or deeds to those around us, or like gossiping about others, or even the common sin of overeating.

It is called a *secret sin* because we are too ashamed to let anyone know we are struggling with it, especially anyone in the church! What a sad case when we can't turn for help to the church because we feel condemned.

When I was a young boy, my father had pornography in our home. One of the earliest times I can remember was when my siblings and I got a spanking for *playing doctor*. It might seem harmless when you see five-year-old kids pulling their pants down and rubbing sand on each other's bare bottoms thinking they are playing doctor. But there are evil spiritual forces at work in the fourth dimension. We know that the Word says we don't fight against flesh and blood but against spiritual powers. Those spirits took root in my life as a young child.

> For our struggle is not against flesh and blood, but against the rulers, against the powers, against the world forces of this darkness, against the spiritual forces of wickedness in the heavenly places.
>
> Ephesians 6:12 (NASB)

But we can thank Jesus, we don't have to put up with sin and evil spiritual forces anymore! We need to know what *Grace* did for us before we can walk victory.

Therefore, since the children share in flesh and blood, He Himself likewise also partook of the same, that through death He might render powerless him who had the power of death, that is, the devil.

Hebrews 2:14 (NASB)

Suffice it to say, that I never had been drunk, never tried drugs of any kind, and never was bound by a spirit of gambling. But this *secret sin* of mine never left my life because I never really took serious steps to get rid of it until many years later.

I remembered that a few months before the Ken Copeland Convention in July 2006, I cried out to God and asked him why this problem kept haunting me. I asked him to do whatever it takes to get it out of my life. Sure enough, he did! However, when I asked him "whatever," I never realized what I was about to go through. That's when God exposed this *sin* and it wasn't secret anymore.

I then entered the hardest and loneliest time in my life when I literally became all alone and helpless. I had no one to turn to but God. That's right where he always wanted me (and wants all of us), totally relying on him for everything. My mental state was so bad that I asked my company to transfer me to another job because I could hardly live day to day as a manager of a sales team. God had a plan and proceeded to pull the weeds (sin) out of my life and replant (replace) it with his word.

The first thing he told me to do was tithe my day. So, I would get up very early every day and start by giving him the first tenth of my day and spend two and a half hours with him and his word. I continued that for ten months. He then had me start a devotional in August 2006 and mail it out to a few close friends. It grew to almost fifty people.

I continued the devotional through the writing of this book and it turned out to be instrumental in my writing of this book. God also wanted me to learn how to hear his voice from my *spirit man*. I have learned to listen to that still small voice (intuition) and judge the thoughts against his word (Philippians 4:8).

In October 2006, he told me in my spirit man to start praying for an hour every day according to Romans 8:26–27 and Jude 20. Over the next two days he confirmed it with two other ministries who suggested the same idea.

I started going on an hour walk with the Lord and would continue this for over the next three to four years. That also established a great habit because to this day, whenever I go walking, I subconsciously start praying out loud according to Jude 20.

I was very ashamed of the selfish man I was from twelve years old to fifty years old. Don't get me wrong, I still deal with selfishness every day, but my perspective is different knowing I *choose* to put his Word first place in my life.

For a short time, I fought bitterness to God and I asked God why it took me until I was fifty years old to get me to a point where I could finally totally surrender to him and make him Lord of my life. One of the most important things God would teach me is that just like the apostle Paul; my past belonged to him.

That's when he showed me Paul's testimony (shared a couple pages above, just preceding my testimony). Notice, when Paul was called Saul, he was the worst sinner that ever lived. God is so cool! It sounds just like God to pick and save the worst sinner of all time and have him write most of the New Testament. Now, everyone knows that no sin is too great to keep us from receiving his gift and the richness of his grace. God showed me my past belonged to him just as much as my future. It's *only* because of his *grace* that my present and future are so much better. Since my past had to collide with his grace to change my life for good, my testimony now belongs to him.

One of the most amazing things that happened since making him Lord of my life in July 2006 was when he started to talk to me through numbers. Please enjoy this story of God as *The Chief Mathematician* and my year of Jubilee (fiftieth).

My Story of God's Love Language to Me Through Numbers

I am about to share a testimony of the amazing way our wonderful God has each life ordered and planned out if we would trust in him *totally* and make him Lord of our ways. God started speaking to me in a "language" of numbers way before I realized it. You will notice that I highlight certain numbers below, but note that it wasn't until December 2006 that I saw a pattern and then in February 2007 he told me that he talks to me in numbers because I was a math major. This is not numerology since I don't use numbers to lead or guide me.

God uses numbers often to confirm my direction or moments in my life. He uses numbers sometimes just to show his presence because of the impossibility with the mathematical statistical odds that could possibly occur by chance. His numbers really show how ordered our lives really are.

This is just one example on how God can speak personally to one individual showing all of us that he truly knows the *number* of hairs on our heads. When you study the Bible you will also see the amazing way he uses numbers so precisely. Even the Hebrew alphabet has letters that also have numerical value. From the number of days of creation and ages of generations, God has the universe numerically ordered.

Because he is a loving God he will not be your Lord and Savior without you choosing him. His love is unfailing, and he will always be there trying to reach each of us. I believe God is constantly trying to reach us (talk to us) in many different ways. He wants us to learn how to hear him. He is not mad at us. God is *Love*. All around us, and his creation constantly points us to a wonderful creator.

It is nothing more complicated than that. Can we fathom how such a wonderful God, so intelligent, so full of love, chooses to love us first and sent his son Jesus as a sacrifice just so he could have a relationship with each and every one of us?

I hope my testimony helps you call out to him and let him speak to you and have a truly unique relationship and a love language just for you. To the chief mathematician! Holy, holy, holy is the Lord God almighty.

- On May 22, 1956 (5/22), I was born in a suburb of Detroit Michigan.
- Autumn 1973–Spring of 1974—I was seventeen years old and a senior in high school when I made a confession and asked Jesus to save me.
- In May 1978, I turned twenty two and graduated from the US Coast Guard Academy with a degree in mathematics with high honors.
- On May 22, 2006—I turned fifty years old.
- On July 5, 2006—My life was in a mess and my marriage was falling apart. I turned to God at a

believer's convention. God told me the main reason was because I was full of pride, and I never made him Lord of my life. I was lord of my own life. I turned to him and surrendered all and asked him to not just be my savior but Lord of everything.

- On Oct 8, 2006—One of my best friends and brother in Christ, Dr. John Symes, revealed to me that this is my year of jubilee—because I was set free at fifty.

The Number Fifty-Five

- On July 30, 2006—God used Paula White on her TV show on TBN when she looked into the TV to talk to a man fifty years old, when she said "*that assignment when you were five to keep you messed up when you were fifty.*" Since I just turned fifty years old and ten weeks earlier, it grabbed my attention, and that's all I noticed from her sermon.

  I did not notice anything else she said because I was caught by surprise and asked myself if this was just coincidence or was God using her to talk to me. I did not think about "numbers" other than she was talking about a man my age. (Also note that in her words the numbers of five and fifty add up to be fifty-five.)

- The next day, July 31, 2006—I read a Ken Copeland daily devotional early that morning titled "Don't serve the problem," It meant so much to me so I printed it up and carried it with me all day.

At that time, I did not notice the location in the scripture reference of the Bible verse used for the devotional. Later that night I watched Jesse Duplantis' TV show on TBN. He started to speak to the TV and quoted Isaiah 55.

Suddenly, my spirit literally leaped inside me because I knew he was talking to me— "reading my mail." I still had Ken's devotional in my hands and looked down, and I noticed for the first time this day to see what the reference verse at the bottom of the page. It also was Isaiah 55.

The presence of God was all over me at that moment. He was confirming what he was saying to my *spirit man*. This is what God was saying to me.

Seek ye the Lord while he may be found, call ye upon him while he is near: Let the wicked forsake his way, and the unrighteous man his thoughts: and let him return unto the Lord, and he will have mercy upon him; and to our God, for he will abundantly pardon. For my thoughts are not your thoughts; neither are your ways my ways; says the Lord… So shall my word be that goes forth out of my mouth; it shall not return unto me void, but it shall accomplish that which I please, and it shall prosper in the thing where to I sent it. For you shall go out with joy and be led forth with peace … and it shall be to the Lord for a "name"; for an everlasting sign that shall not be cut off.

Isaiah 55: 6–13(KJV)

- On August 1, 2006—(Note: This is now the third day in a row…) I was watching the Paula White TV show again, and I did not realize that it was a repeat of the same show two days earlier. I was literally glued to the TV hoping to hear more about this fifty year old man and wondering was God speaking about me. Then I heard it again! This time I was prepared and paying closer attention to her every word. This is what she said: *"In other words, all that junk; all that stuff that life cluttered you with, all that noise in your spirit; all that mess the enemy sent against you, that assignment when you were five to keep you messed up when you were fifty. God's getting ready to send a word, and he's going to make you well, and he's going to make you sound, and he's going to make you whole; because* Isaiah 55 *says that the Word cannot return void, but it will prosper that which it is sent too."*

- In late February 2007— The first church I would attend in Houston—(The Worship Center) on the *first* day at service: Pastor Rusty used Isaiah 55 in his sermon.

• December 20–21, 2008—I was scheduled to land in Boston's Logan airport at 8:30 p.m. on Thursday night, December 20. Due to two flight delays, a detour for refueling and snow in Boston, I did not get off the plane until around 3:00 a.m. on Friday morning. When I stepped outside to look for a taxi to take me to my mother's house thirty minutes away, I walked towards a man leaning against his van and asked me if I needed a ride. Asking how much, he replied $55! I guess I was half asleep because I never "noticed" the number fifty-five until after the day was finished when God showed me this was a divine appointment.

Once we were on the way to Mom's house, the Lord spoke to my spirit to give the man a $20 tip. I immediately discerned that this thought was his voice because it was not my flesh or the devil! I quietly spoke to God and said I will do it. Once I purposed in my heart to do so believing I heard from God, then the Lord confirmed it by bringing back to my memory the words from a verse in the Bible that says "…do not render evil for evil, but instead overcome evil by doing good."

I just experience a "travel day in hell," so to speak. God was showing me how to overcome that by doing good for someone else. Later that *same* day, I was downloading some songs on my new cell phone. I discovered that there were about seven to eight verses I could use as ring tones. They all were common verses (John 3:16, Phil 4:19, etc.) except for one... It was Romans 12:21 – *"Don't let evil conquer you, but conquer evil by doing good."*

This was God's second confirmation to me. Later that night I was on the phone with a friend, the Lord had his final and most amazing confirmation. This time he would use numbers again. While I was talking, he opened my eyes and there I saw it. I could hardly believe it! The verse he gave me to speak to me about overcoming an evil travel day was Romans 12:21, which also was the same number as the very date itself, 12/21 (December 21). This was significant because my flight was supposed to land the night before on 12/20. Praise God. Now the $55 cab fare also had meaning!

The Number Thirty-Eight

• Sunday August 20, 2006—(In my former church in California) Pastor Mike shared his sermon from John 5:5 about the man at the pool of Bethesda. Verse 5 says—*A certain man was at the pool of Bethesda with an infirmity* thirty-eight years...*the man was made whole.* As I sat there, God inspired me to do the math and showed me that I was an adult for the same number of 38 years – 38 as adult

+ 12 years as child = 50 years old. (God also showed me that my life was similar to the man at the pool because I was spiritually oppressed for thirty-eight years). However, I did not notice the number fifty-five in John 5:5 because I still did not realize God was speaking to me in numbers. God was now using the numbers thirty-eight and fifty-five together. This is significant and amazing because this is not the first time He would do that.

- On that *same* day, Sunday Aug 20, 2006—Joyce Meyer, on her TV show on TBN, also mentioned about the same man at the pool for thirty-eight years by quoting John 5:5. This was another confirmation tying my life to the man in John 5:5.

- September 5, 2006—(I think the date is also significant because of God's use of John 5 above and using the age of a child five years old in this story below.). I received the Paula White's CD sermon I ordered a few weeks earlier. I finally was able to find out if I ordered the same sermon I heard while watching her TV show on July 30 and August 1.

I only ordered it based on the line she was talking of a man fifty years old, hoping to hear more about her message, believing God was speaking to me. What is amazing is that while I was looking for the quote I heard on TV, she laid the foundation of her sermon by starting in John 5, just like my pastor did three weeks earlier.

Even more amazing was the way she did it. She first read all six verses in John 5:1–6. She then went back to verse 1 and talked about why her assignment tonight was not about verse 1. She repeated this same thing for verses 2 to 4 and then she skipped 5 and went to 6. Each time saying that her assignment tonight was not about that verse. Then she commented to the audience how she carefully skipped over verse 5. (Verse 5 says – *A certain man was at the pool of Bethesda with an infirmity thirty-eight years ... the man was made whole*). She then said this ..."John 5:5 is the focus of our faith where it says "and there was a certain man there"...are you there?" She shouted slowly and repeatedly a few times... "*Are—You—There*! ... there is the house of mercy ... the house of grace." There is even more amazing things from this sermon that you can read about below in my section dated December 2006.

- On September 15, 2006—While watching Joyce Meyer TV, she said "don't let your problems defeat you—you defeat them. If you don't deal with your problems, sooner or later they will deal with you. Don't be like the crippled man in John 5:5 who dealt with a problem thirty-eight years later."

- On October 16, 2006—While watching Joyce Meyer TV, she said, "It's never too late to get on the path God has ordained for you." She spoke of an IBM engineer for thirty-eight years hating what he did. "It's never too late to do what God planned for you. Take back everything stolen from you."

- In December 2006—Because Paula's sermon was full of messages that were speaking to me; I decided to transcribe her ninety minute sermon. I wanted to be able to mark the time she said certain things, and then I could go back quickly to listen to those areas God was speaking to me through her ministry. I was on the phone this time with my dear friend, Dr. Symes, and I was sharing with him how God seemed to be using numbers to speak to me. This is the time frame that I realized this, and I only noticed the numbers God was using to speak to me since July 2006 were the numbers five, thirty-eight and fifty-five.

    Then I saw it! I had a new revelation and miracle while on the phone with John. I stuttered and was literally speechless on the phone and John kept asking me what was wrong? As I said above, I labeled the time on the CD that Paula said certain things. I had recorded the time in minute: second's format and I specifically recorded the part of the sermon that started this whole journey way back when I first saw Paula preach on TV in July 2006.

Again, she said: "*In other words, all that junk; all that stuff that life cluttered you with, all that noise in your spirit; all that mess the enemy sent against you, that assignment when you were five to keep you messed up when you were fifty. God's getting ready to send a word and he's going to make you well, and he's going to make you sound, and He's going to make you whole; because Isaiah 55 says that the Word cannot return void, but it will prosper that which it is sent too*". The minute and second into her sermon when she said that was minute thirty eight and fifty-five second.. I listed it on my notes as 38:55! This was amazing!

- On January 7, 2007—While watching Jerry Savelle on TV, he said, "This is going to be the best year of your life." In 2007 you are going to be the winner God has called you to be. Joy is a spiritual force. Jerry said his ministry was turning thirty-eight years old. This is significant because Jerry's ministry would play a key role to me in many ways in 2006 and 2007.

By the end of 2006, the only numbers God used in my life for the last six months were five, thirty-eight and fifty-five. It wasn't until after God made it clear to me that he was speaking to me in a very unique and personal way by using these three numbers, then he started using other numbers to continue to bless me.

The mathematical odds of these events are practically impossible. God's sole purpose was to confirm his presence and his desire to talk with me and show me how awesome He really is. Do you think anyone of us could write a script like this? What follows are some other numbers and how he used them.

The Number Twenty-Two

- Week covering February 14, 2007—This was the first time I was aware of him using this number. Please note my birthday is on the twenty second. God would follow my lead on this one. When I planned a business trip to Philadelphia via a layover in Houston, I decided to pick my seats on row twenty-two.

   However, I could only do it for three of the four flights. Also, I did not pick them because I expected God to follow my lead. I liked the number so I picked my airplane seats with seats numbered twenty-two. I had no expectations. On the *only* flight that I was not able to pick row twenty-two, the plane pulled into gate twenty-two! When I arrived at the hotel I was given room number 1122. I would routinely watch only one main channel on TV when I traveled which was the channel for Fox news.

Guess what channel it was on during this trip? You guessed it! It was on channel twenty-two. I also had a business associate who forgot to pack some white gym socks. I had an extra pair and offered to loan them to her. When I asked her what room to bring them to, she said 1022. On the flight home (in row 22) I watched a movie about a man in the Coast Guard just like my past whose wife left him also like my situation. He saved many lives in his job and was asked a few times in the movie how many lives he saved; he would always avoid the answer until the end of the movie. When he was finally asked to tell how many people he saved, he answered with the number twenty-two. I definitely saw God doing something. I asked God what was going on and he spoke to me in my heart that he was talking to me in numbers because I am a math major and that was a language I liked to use.

The Number 188

- My PO Box for four years at US Coast Guard Academy was 188.

- Since 2002, my cell phone number has ended with the four numbers of 1188.

- April 2007—I went to see the Andrew Wommack conference in Houston. Andrew Wommack delivered a sermon that I realized was meant for me when he started the sermon by stating Moses wrote 188 chapters in the Bible. Why would God have Andy say 188 chapters when it is easier to say Moses wrote "The Torah," or he wrote the first 5 books of the Bible? Chapters were put in the Bible by man.

It doesn't make sense why Andrew would use that number? It caught my attention, and that allowed the Holy Spirit to tell me, *"Listen up, Scott. This message is for you!"* Andrew taught on lessons we can learn from Moses' life. Specifically, his message was about knowing the timing of God's will is just as important as knowing the calling on your life.

Humans have a tendency to not want to wait on God but run ahead. God therefore caught my attention with this number 188. Like Moses failed to do, I needed to wait on God for the fulfillment of my calling, restoration, and coming out of my personal spiritual wilderness.

Moses was in his wilderness for forty years. The Jewish traditional age for a boy becoming a man is after his twelfth birthday. On May 22, 2008, I turned fifty two years old. Like Moses's forty years in the wilderness, I would be forty years as an adult since my twelfth birthday.

- My all-time favorite movie has always been the 1981 Academy Award winning film, *Chariots of Fire*. It's about my hero, Eric Liddell, who literally ran for God's glory. In the movie, there is a scene where the number of paces around the quadrangle was 188 paces.

- In 2008, I would get a new company car. My vehicle had a license plate with both letters and numbers. The only three numbers and in sequence were 188. I would have this vehicle when I would meet my future wife. That is significant now that I look back on it because 188 was the number God would use to teach me to listen and "wait" on him for restoration in my life and not try to make it happen myself.

- In December 2008, God would confirm my target body weight at 188 pounds.

- On a side note, the very middle verse in the Bible is Psalms 118:8. There are 594 chapters before Psalms 118 and 594 chapters after it for a total of 1188 chapters. This is just one example of Gods perfect order to his word, not to mention confirm to me the order he has for my life.

The Number Thirty-Three

- November 4, 2007—Only days after a recent and very emotional experience, I questioned God if I was really in his will and supposed to be living in Houston. I was walking up my driveway after returning from a jog, God would lead me by dropping the thought into my spirit to "Add up the numbers!"

  I understood immediately what to do. I added the numbers of my birthday with my street address in Houston. When I added my street address of 33 to my birthday 5/22 it came out to be 38/55! *Wow!* This is the *exact same* number for the location on the CD of Paula White's message about me. I explained this above where it was timed at min:sec of 38:55. Could anyone write this story other than God? Also note how God followed this up with another confirmation of this on November 5 as seen below with number 5/22.

- Two weeks later, for the whole week covering November 19, 2007—During this week of Thanksgiving, God would now confirm to me the number thirty-three one time each day. I saw it while I was driving on a huge billboard or on the screen of my XM radio, etc. He now was confirming my house number 33 which He used on November

4, 2007 (above) to confirm to me that I was meant to be exactly where I was at that time in Houston, Texas.

- In 2009, I would run a 5K race with a dear friend, Chris who lost his leg in an accident the year before. I would do this only for two consecutive years. I placed thirty-third on the first year and then would place twenty-second on the next year.

- April 5, 2009—I would become engaged to my future wife when she was still thirty-three years old.

The Number of My Birthday 5/22

- November 5, 2007—(Note this is literally the *next day* after events from November 4) —I went jogging from my house to a 1 kilometer jogging track nearby. I started my stopwatch in the street at a random spot in front of my home. When I arrived at the jogging track, I looked down at my stopwatch to see how long it took me to get there and it was 5:22.

  Then after making one complete lap around the 1 kilometer track, I looked at my watch again and noticed the time elapsed was 10:44 (or another 5:22 had elapsed). I thought it was a cool coincidence and never thought about it again … until after I finished my run. After completing three more laps and then running home, I stopped running at another random spot in the street near my house. I then stopped my watch when the Lord said *"add it up."* I looked at the time of 32:12.

That was *exactly* equal to six times the time of 5:22. I felt overwhelmed! I could hear God speak softly to me, and he said, Scott, *"your life is marked, it is perfectly ordered!"* There is significance and order in the way God did this too. The first time he gave me 38:55 was a min/sec amount of time. Then he used the same 38/55 to tie my birthday into it, and then he went back to using my birthday as time in min:sec format. Awesome is the Lord God Almighty!

- January 1, 2008—God also led me to set my phone alarm for 5:22 a.m. to start my day with him. Little did I know what would happen days later.

- January 5, 2008—I returned home from a two-week vacation. I noticed that my "old fashioned coil windup" alarm clock had randomly stopped at exactly 5:22. I set the alarm for 5:22 the day I left for vacation. It would tick away for hours until it finally stopped long after I was gone. It would stop on the time of 5:22.

   This was absolutely amazing because when you wind up an old fashioned alarm clock you have no idea where the clock will stop working once the wound mechanism is finished. This is just another of God's ways of saying he is ordering my life. I set the "alarm" hand and he set the hour/minute hands.

The Number Forty

- April 2007—As mentioned above, when I was at the Andrew Wommack conference in Houston, I learned how Moses was led to the wilderness for forty years after he killed the Egyptian because he presumed it was time for God to fulfill his calling. God would use this to explain to me that my wilderness would end after forty years from my twelfth birthday.

That means that at some time after May 22 in the year 2008, I would be led out into my calling for the rest of my life. That is what I believed the Spirit of God was saying to me. God was also teaching me that it was just as important to know the timing of God's will as it was of what his calling would be for your life.

Moses is a good example of that message. Remember, that God told me to pay attention to this sermon when Andrew mentioned 188 chapters. Well, just months after my fifty-second birthday, God would bring me together with my future wife Rachel and my restoration he promised from after my year of Jubilee in 2006.

- Late 2007—For a few times since the April Wommack conference, I would think about the number 188, and if there was more meaning to that number. I thought that since 5/22 and 33 add up to 38/55 that there might be some similar combination with 188. Despite my thoughts, I could not figure out or see any combination. God kept my eyes darkened on this until January 2008.

- January 22, 2008—After trying many times to figure out if there were other mathematical meanings behind the number 188, the Lord led me to try again. This time my eyes were opened. And it was on January 22 too! Amazing.

  So what were my eyes opened to, you ask? Remember that God gave me the number 188 at the sermon about Moses and how God said that I would be in my wilderness for forty years. Well, when I subtracted 22, 33, 38, and 55 from 188 I was left with 40! Praise God. He was confirming exactly what he said to me and doing so on January 22.

A Story of the Number and Verse in Isaiah 41:13

- In December 2008. While on a vacation break, I received a very disturbing call from my boss about a situation at work. It caused me great stress just a couple days before Christmas and could have spoiled my holiday. That night I spent some time in the Word and God led me to a promise for me for that very important moment.

For I the Lord your God hold your right hand; I am the Lord, Who says to you, Fear not; I will help you.

Isaiah 41:13 (AMP)

The very next morning I went to the gym. I got on the treadmill and set the time for sixty minutes. Sometime after starting, I accidently hit the emergency stop button. I noticed the number of calories I burned was 187. I said to God, almost in an unhappy tone, "why couldn't you have stopped this at 188?" Then I heard his voice inside me say subtract the time. The time on the treadmill had stopped at 18:47. When I hit the button on the machine to switch from the *time elapsed* to *time remaining*, it would change it to 41:13! That was exactly the same as the verse in Isaiah God gave to me the night before. He just wanted me to know by confirming that he indeed was speaking to me because I was still fighting off doubts and worry. Do you think I was worried anymore? This is another perfect example of God using numbers to confirm something He already told me the night before. Numbers were not guiding me. Numbers were confirming.

The story of 7 and 11 (7/11)

- Sunday, February 22, 2009—While on my hour long prayer walk, God would speak again to my *spirit man*. I was praying about my relationship with Rachel and I heard him say to me as clear as bell, "Get married on 7/11." I had to stop and judge what just happened. I looked at the calendar on my phone and sure enough, July 11, 2009 was on a Saturday. Surely, this *could* be another voice saying that to me, right? Well, later that morning I was in church sitting in a pew with my girlfriend, Rachel. Pastor Frankie opened his sermon up by stating that his message would be easy to remember because it was taken from two different verses— and he said the words—verses "seven and eleven." I almost turned white and turned my head to Rachel like I saw a ghost!

  She asked me, what's the matter? I then cracked a smile and said I would have to tell her later. Again, God was confirming something he said to my spirit on my walk that morning. Numbers were not guiding me. Numbers were confirming.

The Number 2228

On December 11, 2012, I received a phone call from my book publisher explaining to me that he wanted to publish this book. It was late afternoon and as I was driving my car out of a parking lot, I noticed that license plate of the car in front of me. It had these for numbers, 2228. I thought it was cool to see 222 because of the number 22 in my life but also because God told me to marry Rachel when I was on a prayer walk on 2/22 in 2009. But God had a bigger message for me. Just a couple hours later my wife and I stopped by a store on the way to the gym. We purchased four items and the bill was $22.28! The odds of that occurring were 1 in 10,000 alone. But God was not finished. After about thirty to thirty-five minutes on the treadmill, I decided to slow down to end my session, and as I went to push the controls I noticed the distance I walked was 2.22 miles!

And once I got home, I proceeded to enter my miles driven that day in my logbook and I noticed that I started my day as 22,270. I kind of jokingly complained to God and said "why didn't you make so my day started with an odometer of 22,280?"

He quickly responded back to me in my understanding that it didn't matter because I did pass the 22,280 mile mark during that day. Finally, it was shared with me that the numerical value of 2228 is 5 which is the number for

Grace, which is what this book is all about. (2+2+2+8 =14 and 1+4 =5)

Stories like this continue to occur in my life. They are numerous. God is so personal with all of us in the ways he wants to show his glory, wisdom, and presence. My hope is that you will take with you the message of the richness of his grace. He wants to have a meaningful personal relationship with each of you. He wants to talk to each of you in a unique and personal way.

INTRODUCTION

Ten Important Definitions

Complete

And in Him you have been made complete, and He is the head over all rule and authority.

Colossians 2:10 (NASB)

1. having all parts or elements; lacking nothing; whole; entire; full: *a complete set.*
2. finished; ended; concluded: *a complete orbit.*
3. having all the required or customary characteristics, skills, or the like; consummate; perfect in kind or quality.
4. thorough; entire; total; undivided, uncompromised, or unmodified: *a complete victory;*

Finished

> Therefore when Jesus had received the sour wine, He said, "It is finished!" And He bowed His head and gave up His spirit.
>
> John 19:30 (NASB)

1. ended or completed.
2. completed or perfected in all details, as a product: *to pack and ship finished items.*

Forever

> Therefore He is able also to save forever those who draw near to God through Him, since He always lives to make intercession for them.
>
> Hebrews 7:25 (NASB)

1. without ever ending; eternally: *to last forever.*
2. continually; incessantly; always.

Free

> But the free gift is not like the transgression. For if by the transgression of the one the many died, much more did the grace of God and the gift by the grace of the one Man, Jesus Christ, abound to the many.
>
> Romans 5:15 (NASB)

1. pertaining to or reserved for those who enjoy personal liberty
2. exempt from external authority, interference, restriction, etc., as a person or one's will, thought, choice, action, etc.; independent; unrestricted.

Gift

> But the free gift is not like the transgression. For if by the transgression of the one the many died, much more did the grace of God and the gift by the grace of the one Man, Jesus Christ, abound to the many.
>
> Romans 5:15 (NASB)

1. something given voluntarily without payment in return, as to show favor toward someone, honor an occasion, or make a gesture of assistance; present.
2. something bestowed or acquired without any particular effort by the recipient or without its being earned.

Heir

> Therefore you are no longer a slave, but a son; and if a son, then an heir through God.
>
> Galatians 4:7 (NASB)

1. a person who inherits all the property of a deceased person, as by descent, relationship, will, or, legal process.
2. a person who inherits or is entitled to inherit the rank, title, position, etc., of another.

Inheritance

…giving thanks to the Father who has qualified us to share in the inheritance of the saints in light.

Colossians 1:12 (NASB)

1. something, as a quality, characteristic, or other immaterial possession received from progenitors or predecessors as if by succession: *an inheritance of family pride.*
2. portion; birthright; heritage: *Absolute rule was considered the inheritance of kings.*

Perfect

For by that one offering he forever made perfect those who are sanctified.

Hebrews 10:14 (NLT)

1. conforming absolutely to the description or definition of an ideal type: *a perfect sphere.*

2. excellent or complete beyond practical or theoretical improvement: *There is no perfect legal code. The proportions of this temple are almost perfect.*
3. entirely without any flaws, defects, or shortcomings: *a perfect apple.*
4. accurate, exact, or correct in every detail: *a perfect copy.*

Promise

> For if the inheritance is based on law, it is no longer based on a promise; but God has granted it to Abraham by means of a promise.
>
> Galatians 3:18 (NASB)

1. a declaration that something will or will not be done, given, etc., by one:
2. an express assurance on which expectation is to be based:
3. something that has the effect of an express assurance; indication of what may be expected.

Qualified

> …giving thanks to the Father who has qualified us to share in the inheritance of the saints in light.
>
> Colossians 1:12 (NASB)

1. having the qualities, accomplishments, etc., required by law or custom for getting, having, or exercising a right, holding an office, or the like.

All definitions came from www.dictionary.com

Spirit, Soul, and Body

Now may the God of peace Himself sanctify you entirely; and may your spirit and soul and body be preserved complete, without blame at the coming of our Lord ...

1 Thessalonians 5:23 (NASB)

Jesus answered and said to him, "Truly, truly, I say to you, unless one is born again he cannot see the kingdom of God."

Nicodemus said to Him, "How can a man be born when he is old? He cannot enter a second time into his mother's womb and be born, can he?" Jesus answered, "Truly, truly, I say to you, unless one is born of water and the Spirit he cannot enter into the kingdom of God. That which is born of the flesh is flesh, and that which is born of the Spirit is spirit.

John 3:3–6 (NASB)

When we become born again like Jesus shared with Nicodemus above, our spirit is changed instantly. We accept that by faith because our physical senses and body do not change.

> If Christ is in you, though the body is dead because of sin, yet the spirit is alive because of righteousness.
>
> Romans 8:10 (NASB)

This topic is significant in understanding *grace* because it is easy for us to think about ourselves only in terms of our body and mind (emotions and soul), and forget that our *real* person is our *spirit man* who never dies. God is a spirit (1 John 4:24). The realm of the spirit world is more real than our physical world since everything created in our three dimensions originated from God's fourth dimension of the spirit (Colossians 1:16).

Our *spirit man* is the most significant and important part of our triune being. We can easily miss that the Word may be actually talking about our *spirit man* when we think it is talking about our soul and body. Understanding these differences will help you understand the message of grace.

Spirit

> To the general assembly and church of the firstborn, who are enrolled in heaven, and to God, the Judge of all, and to the spirits of the righteous made perfect.
>
> Hebrews 12:23 (NASB)

giving thanks to the Father, who has qualified us to share in the inheritance of the saints in Light. For He rescued us from the domain of darkness, and transferred us to the kingdom of His beloved Son,

Colossians 1:12–13 (NASB)

And baptism, which is a figure [of their deliverance], does now also save you [from inward questionings and fears], not by the removing of outward body filth [bathing], but by [providing you with] the answer of a good and clear conscience (inward cleanness and peace) before God [because you are demonstrating what you believe to be yours] through the resurrection of Jesus Christ.

1 Peter 3:21 (AMP)

Having been buried with Him in baptism, in which you were also raised up with Him through faith in the working of God, who raised Him from the dead…He made you alive together with Him, having forgiven us all our transgressions, having canceled out the certificate of debt consisting of decrees against us, which was hostile to us; and He has taken it out of the way, having nailed it to the cross.

Colossians 2:12–14 (NASB)

Soul and Body

Corresponding to that, baptism now saves you [spirit]—not the removal of dirt from the flesh [body], but an appeal to God for a good conscience [soul]—through the resurrection of Jesus Christ,

1Peter 3:21 (NASB)

Are you so foolish? Having begun by the Spirit, are you now being perfected by the flesh (body)?

Galatians 3:3 (NASB)

For while we were in the flesh (body), the sinful passions, which were aroused by the Law, were at work in the members of our body to bear fruit for death.

Romans 7:5 (NASB)

But I see a different law in the members of my body, waging war against the law of my mind [soul], and making me a prisoner of the law of sin which is in my members [body].

Romans 7:23 (NASB)

Walk by the Spirit, and you will not carry out the desire of the flesh [body]. For the flesh [body] sets its desires against the Spirit, and the spirit against the flesh [body]; for these are in opposition to one another…

Galatians 5:16-18 (NASB)

Finally, I'd like to share three analogies I believe could help us better understand the difference between our *spirit man* and our physical flesh.

First analogy: Consider all the automobiles the average person owns in his or her lifetime. Let's just say it's around ten. Does your earthly father (or mother) see you as your car or the person inside it? When they want to communicate with you, do they speak to your car or your person inside the car? If your car is a wreck, scratched up, or not working properly, does that change who you really are or how your earthly father sees you? Likewise, God is a spirit and the real you are a spirit living in a body (*car*) and God saves your spirit once you become born again.

Second analogy: Consider the apartments or homes you have lived your whole life. Similar to the questions above about a car, does your home represent you or is it just the dwelling you live in? Likewise, your spirit lives in an earthly home called a body. That body is needed to live in these three dimensions on this planet.

Third analogy: If you wanted to walk on the moon you would need a space suit. That suit is not you at all. It allows you to "live" on the moon's surface. Likewise our body is a spacesuit for our spirit in order for us to live on this planet.

THE LAW AND
WORKS OF MAN

An Allegory: Children of the promise

The Scriptures say that Abraham had two sons, one from his slave wife and one from his freeborn wife. The son of the slave wife was born in a human attempt to bring about the fulfillment of God's promise. But the son of the freeborn wife was born as God's own fulfillment of his promise. These two women serve as an illustration of God's two covenants. The first woman, Hagar, represents Mount Sinai where people received the law that enslaved them. And now Jerusalem is just like Mount Sinai in Arabia, because she and her children live in slavery to the law. But the other woman, Sarah, represents the heavenly Jerusalem. She is the free woman, and she is our mother.

As Isaiah said,

"Rejoice, O childless woman, you who have never given birth!

Break into a joyful shout, you who have never been in labor!

For the desolate woman now has more children than the woman who lives with her husband!"

And you, dear brothers and sisters, are children of the promise, just like Isaac. But you are now being persecuted by those who want you to keep the law, just as Ishmael, the child born by human effort, persecuted Isaac, the child born by the power of the Spirit.

But what do the Scriptures say about that? "Get rid of the slave and her son, for the son of the slave woman will not share the inheritance with the free woman's son." So, dear brothers and sisters, we are not children of the slave woman; we are children of the free woman.

Galatians 4:22–31 (NASB)

The Apostle Paul just stated that believers through faith in Christ are children of the free woman, children of the promised blessing, and heirs with Abraham apart from the law. (Reviewing the definitions—promise is an express assurance on which expectation is to be based; an inheritance is a birthright; heritage.)

The Law is the Ministry of Death

Not that we are adequate in ourselves to consider anything as coming from ourselves, but our adequacy is from God, who also made us adequate as servants of a new covenant, not of the letter but of the Spirit; for the letter kills, but the Spirit gives life. But if the ministry of death, in letters engraved on stones, came with glory, so that the sons of Israel could not look intently at the face of Moses because of the glory of his face, fading as it was, how will the ministry of the Spirit fail to be even more with glory? For if the ministry of condemnation has glory, much more does the ministry of righteousness abound in glory.

2 Corinthians 3:5–9 (NASB)

The law given to Moses could only lead God's people toward death.

The Law Provides the Power to Sin

The sting of death is sin, and the power of sin is the law.

1 Corinthians 15:56 (NASB)

For through the Law comes the knowledge of sin.

Romans 3:20–21 (NASB)

Where Is the Boasting for All Your Efforts?

> Therefore, [inheriting] the promise is the outcome of faith and depends [entirely] on faith, in order that it might be given as an act of grace (unmerited favor), to make it stable and valid and guaranteed to all his descendants—not only to the devotees and adherents of the Law, but also to those who share the faith of Abraham, who is [thus] the father of us all.
>
> Romans 4:16 (AMP)

> For it is by free grace (God's unmerited favor) that you are saved (delivered from judgment and made partakers of Christ's salvation) through [your] faith. And this [salvation] is not of yourselves [of your own doing, it came not through your own striving], but it is the gift of God.
>
> Ephesians 2:8 (AMP)

> Where then is boasting? It is excluded. By what kind of law? Of works? No, but by a law of faith.
>
> Romans 3:27 (NASB)

The Promise that Came after the Law

For the Law appoints men as high priests who are weak, but the word of the oath [promise], which came after the Law, appoints a Son, made perfect forever.

Hebrews 7:28 (NASB)

or

For the Law sets up men in their weakness [frail, sinful, dying human beings] as high priests, but the word of [God's] oath, which [was spoken later] after the institution of the Law, [chooses and appoints as priest One Whose appointment is complete and permanent], a Son Who has been made perfect forever.

Hebrews 7:28 (AMP)

And now I commend you to God and to the word of His grace, which is able to build you up and to give you the inheritance among all those who are sanctified.

Acts 20:32 (NASB)

Conclusion #1

Inheriting the promise doesn't come from obeying the law, but it depends entirely on faith (Romans 4:16 above), in order that the promise can be given as a free gift of grace (unmerited favor). (Ephesians 2:8) (Reviewing definitions for free gift—exempt from external authority, interference, restriction for something given voluntarily without payment in return.)

The Law Was Only a Shadow of Reality to Come

The old system under the Law of Moses was only a shadow, a dim preview of the good things to come, not the good things themselves. The sacrifices under that system were repeated again and again, year after year, but they were never able to provide perfect cleansing for those who came to worship. If they could have provided perfect cleansing, the sacrifices would have stopped, for the worshipers would have been purified once for all time, and their feelings of guilt would have disappeared. But instead, those sacrifices actually reminded them of their sins year after year

Hebrews 10:1–3 (NLT)

They serve in a system of worship that is only a copy, a shadow of the real one in heaven. For when Moses was getting ready to build the Tabernacle, God gave him this warning: "Be sure that you make everything according to the pattern I have shown you here on the mountain."

Hebrews 8:5 (NLT)

For these rules are only shadows of the reality yet to come. And Christ himself is that reality.

Colossians 2:17 (NLT)

Dead Works and Lifeless Observances

Therefore leaving the elementary teaching about the Christ, let us press on to maturity, not laying again a foundation of repentance from dead works and of faith toward God.

Hebrews 6:1 (NASB)

How much more will the blood of Christ, who through the eternal Spirit offered Himself without blemish to God, cleanse your conscience from dead works to serve the living God?

Hebrews 9:14 (NASB)

Who has saved us and called us with a holy calling, not according to our works, but according to His ... grace which was granted us in Christ Jesus from all eternity.

2 Timothy 1:9 (NASB)

Yet we know that a man is justified or reckoned righteous and in right standing with God not by works of the Law, but [only] through faith ... [Therefore] even we [ourselves] have believed on Christ Jesus, in order to be justified by faith in Christ and not by works of the Law [for we cannot be justified by any observance of the ritual of the Law given by Moses], because by keeping legal rituals and by works no human being can ever be justified (declared righteous and put in right standing with God).

Galatians 2:16 (AMP)

And so you cancel the word of God in order to hand down your own tradition. And this is only one example among many others."

Mark 7:13 (NLT)

He calls people, but not according to their good or bad works…

Romans 9:12 (NLT)

Conclusion #2

The law can never make anyone perfect. (Review of the definition for perfect—entirely without any flaws, defects, or shortcomings.) Notice Romans 9:12 includes the words "good works," too! So, why do we try so hard to be accepted by God with our efforts or actions? Why do we expect God to count these "good" Christian works towards our salvation?

The Only Obedience that Really Mattered

God's promise to give the whole earth to Abraham and his descendants was based not on his obedience to God's law, but on a right relationship with God that comes by faith.

Romans 4:13 (NLT)

Because one person disobeyed God, many became sinners. But because one other person obeyed God, many will be made righteous.

Romans 5:19 (NLT)

… Jesus Christ, the faithful witness, the firstborn of the dead, and the ruler of the kings of the earth. To Him who loves us and released us from our sins by His blood.

Revelation 1:5 (NASB)

Written on Their hearts

When Gentiles who have not the [divine] Law do instinctively what the Law requires, they are a law to themselves, since they do not have the Law. They show that the essential requirements of the Law are written in their hearts and are operating there, with which their consciences (sense of right and wrong) also bear witness; and their [moral] decisions (their arguments of reason, their condemning or approving thoughts) will accuse or perhaps defend and excuse [them]. On that day when, as my Gospel proclaims, God by Jesus Christ will judge men in regard to the things which they conceal (their hidden thoughts).

Romans 2:14–16 (AMP)

Because by the works of the Law, no flesh will be justified in His sight; for through the Law comes the knowledge of sin.

Romans 3:20–21 (NASB)

Conclusion #3

The law is of no value for our salvation (righteousness). It does have value in directing our lives for success and blessings.

But if you look carefully into the perfect law that sets you free, and if you do what it says and don't forget what you heard, then God will bless you for doing it.

James 1:25 (NLT)

Our acceptance with God comes only through Jesus who was the only one who fulfilled the law perfectly for us. With or without the law, everyone (including those never taught the law of God) instinctively knows the difference between right and wrong.

Your own Religious Plans and Projects

Is it not clear to you that to go back to that old rule-keeping, peer-pleasing religion would be an abandonment of everything personal and free in my relationship with God? I refuse to do that, to repudiate God's grace. If a living relationship with God could come by rule-keeping, then Christ died unnecessarily.

Galatians 2:21 (MSG)

I suspect you would never intend this, but this is what happens. When you attempt to live by your own religious plans and projects, you are cut off from Christ, you fall out of grace. Meanwhile we expectantly wait for a satisfying relationship with the Spirit. For in Christ, neither our most conscientious religion nor disregard of religion amounts to anything.

Galatians 5:4 (MSG)

Can We Be Accepted by God through Our Works?

But suppose we seek to be made right with God through faith in Christ, and then we are found guilty because we have abandoned the law. Would that mean Christ has led us into sin? Absolutely not!

Galatians 2:17 (NLT)

or

As we try to become right with God by what Christ has done for us, what if we find we are sinners also? Does that mean Christ makes us sinners? No! Never!

Galatians 2:17 (NLT)

No Longer Driven to Impress God

Have some of you noticed that we [physical body] are not yet perfect? (No great surprise, right?) And are you ready to make the accusation that since people like me, who go through Christ in order to get things right with God, aren't perfectly virtuous, Christ must therefore be an accessory to sin? The accusation is frivolous.

If I was "trying to be good," I would be rebuilding the same old barn that I tore down. I would be acting as a charlatan. What actually took place is this: I tried keeping rules and working my head off to please God, and it didn't work. So I quit being a "law man" so that I could be God's man. Christ's life showed me how, and enabled me to do it. I identified myself completely with him. Indeed, I have been crucified with Christ. My ego is no longer central. It is no longer important that I appear righteous before you or have your good opinion, and I am no longer driven to impress God. Christ lives in me.

The life you see me living is not "mine," but it is lived by faith in the Son of God, who loved me and gave himself for me. I am not going to go back on that. Is it not clear to you that to go back to that old rule-keeping, peer-pleasing religion would be an abandonment of everything personal and free in my relationship with God? I refuse to do that, to repudiate God's grace. If a living relationship with

God could come by rule-keeping, then Christ died unnecessarily.

Galatians 2:17–21 (MSG)

He calls people, but not according to their good or bad works …

Romans 9:12 (NLT)

Conclusion #4

We cannot impress or please God as Christians by any effort we put forth to obey God's law. It is impossible to please God without faith. (Hebrews 11:6). He wants us to please him by putting our faith in his free gift of grace (something given voluntarily without payment in return) through and from Jesus. It's not about our efforts anymore; good or bad.

A Wicked Man Who Prolongs His Life

For we have all become like one who is unclean …, and all our righteousness (our best deeds of rightness and justice) is like filthy rags or a polluted garment; we all fade like a leaf, and our iniquities, like the wind, take us away [far from God's favor, hurrying us toward destruction].

Isaiah 64:6 (NASB)

I have seen everything in the days of my vanity (my emptiness, falsity, vainglory, and futility): there is a righteous man who perishes in his righteousness, and there is a wicked man who prolongs his life in spite of his evildoing.

Ecclesiastes 7:15 (NASB)

He calls people, but not according to their good or bad works...

Romans 9:12 (NLT)

A Business Deal and Ironclad Contract?

For the promise to Abraham or to his descendants that he would be heir of the world was not through the Law, but through the righteousness of faith. For if those who are of the Law are heirs, faith is made void and the promise is nullified; for the Law brings about wrath, but where there is no law, there also is no violation. For this reason it is by faith, in order that it may be in accordance with grace.

Roman 4:13–16 (NASB)

or

That famous promise God gave Abraham—that he and his children would possess the earth—was not given because of something Abraham did or would do. It was based on God's decision to put everything together for him, which Abraham then entered when he believed. If those who get what God gives them only get it by doing everything they are told to do and filling out all the right forms properly signed, that eliminates personal trust completely and turns the promise into an ironclad contract!

That's not a holy promise; that's a business deal. A contract drawn up by a hard-nosed lawyer and with plenty of fine print only makes sure that you will never be able to collect. But if there is no contract in the first place, simply a promise—and God's promise at that—you can't break it.

Roman 4:13–16 (MSG)

Conclusion #5

You can't break a promise God made! You cannot be an heir (a person who inherits or is entitled to inherit the rank, title, position, etc., of another) with Abraham by following the law and rules. It has to be only by faith so that it can be by grace.

Cut off from Christ and Fallen from God's Grace

You have been severed from Christ, you who are seeking to be justified by law; you have fallen from grace. For we, through the Spirit, by faith, are waiting for the hope of righteousness. For in Christ Jesus neither circumcision nor uncircumcision means anything, but faith working through love.

Galatians 5:4 (NASB)

or

I suspect you would never intend this, but this is what happens. When you attempt to live by your own religious plans and projects, you are cut off from Christ, you fall out of grace. Meanwhile we expectantly wait for a satisfying relationship with the Spirit. For in Christ, neither our most conscientious religion nor disregard of religion amounts to anything. What matters is something far more interior: faith expressed in love.

Galatians 5:4 (MSG)

Then note and appreciate the gracious kindness and the severity of God: severity toward those who have fallen, but God's gracious kindness to you—provided you continue in His grace and abide in His kindness; otherwise you too will be cut off (pruned away).

Romans 11:22 (AMP)

… see that no one falls back from and fails to secure God's grace (His unmerited favor and spiritual blessing),

Hebrews 12:15 (AMP)

We have obtained our introduction by faith into this grace.

Romans 5:2 (NASB)

Did Christ Die in Vain?

[Therefore, I do not treat God's gracious gift as something of minor importance and defeat its very purpose]; I do not set aside and invalidate and frustrate and nullify the grace (unmerited favor) of God. For if justification (righteousness, acquittal from guilt) comes through [observing the ritual of] the Law, then Christ (the Messiah) died groundlessly and to no purpose and in vain. [His death was then wholly superfluous.]

Galatians 2:21 (AMP)

But suppose we seek to be made right with God through faith in Christ and then we are found guilty because we have abandoned the law. Would that mean Christ has led us into sin? Absolutely not!

Galatians 2:17 (NLT)

How to Continue in His Grace

But God's gracious kindness to you—provided you continue in His grace ...

Romans 11:22 (AMP)

But if it is by grace, it is no longer on the basis of works; otherwise grace is no longer grace.

Romans 11:6 (NASB)

For this reason it is by faith, so that it may be in accordance with grace.

Romans 4:16 (NASB)

'Are you so foolish…'

… fools die for lack of understanding.

Proverbs 10:21 (AMP)

Therefore do not be vague and thoughtless and foolish, but understanding and firmly grasping what the will of the Lord is.

Ephesians 5:17 (AMP)

Let me ask you this one question: Did you receive the [Holy] Spirit as the result of obeying the Law and doing its works, or was it by hearing [the message of the Gospel] and believing [it]? [Was it from observing a law of rituals or from a message of faith?] Are you so foolish and so senseless and so silly? Having begun [your new life spiritually] with the [Holy] Spirit, are you now reaching perfection [by dependence] on the flesh?

Galatians 3:2–3 (AMP)

But avoid stupid and foolish controversies and genealogies and dissensions and wrangling about the Law, for they are unprofitable and futile.

Titus 3:9 (AMP)

Conclusion #6

Paul makes it clear that trying to please God by your efforts to obey his laws actually frustrate the work of Christ. That would mean that Christ died in vain. This is a critical point in understanding God's free gift of grace and when Jesus said "it is finished" on the cross, there was and is nothing more that needs to be done to put us in any better standing with God. This is an anathema to many in the church, those that insist that once you are saved you still have to live by some kind of law to keep your salvation. Paul speaks about this in Romans 4 and we will address this argument in chapter dealing with common arguments.

Aliens, Slaves, and Strangers

> So then you are no longer strangers and aliens, but you are fellow citizens with the saints, and are of God's household.
>
> Ephesians 2:19 (NASB)

> Therefore you are no longer a slave, but a son; and if a son, then an heir through God.
>
> Galatians 4:7 (NASB)

> For if the inheritance is based on law, it is no longer based on a promise; but God has granted it to Abraham by means of a promise.
>
> Galatians 3:18 (NASB)

For the Law, since it has only a shadow of the good things to come and not the very form of things, can never, by the same sacrifices which they offer continually year by year, make perfect those who draw near. Otherwise, would they not have ceased to be offered, because the worshippers, having once been cleansed, would no longer have had consciousness of sins? But in those sacrifices there is a reminder of sins year by year … Now where there is forgiveness of these things, there is no longer any offering for sin.

Hebrews 10:1–3, 18 (NASB)

The Last Enemy

[It is that purpose and grace] which He now has made known and has fully disclosed and made real [to us] through the appearing of our Savior Christ Jesus, Who annulled death and made it of no effect and brought life and immortality (immunity from eternal death) to light through the Gospel.

2 Timothy 1:10 (AMP)

The last enemy that will be abolished is death.

1 Corinthians 15:26 (NASB)

Therefore when Jesus had received the sour wine, He said, "It is finished!" And He bowed His head and gave up His spirit.

John 19:30 (NASB)

Apart from the Law, Sin is Dead

> But sin, taking opportunity through the commandment, produced in me coveting of every kind; for apart from the Law, sin is dead. I was once alive apart from the Law; but when the commandment came, sin became alive and I died.
>
> Romans 7:8–9 (NASB)

Does this mean that there was no sin from Adam to Moses? Or, at least, was there any consciousness of sin before Moses? ... So, in the next chapter we deal with the subject of sin.

Sin

The sting of death is sin, and the power of sin is the law.

1 Corinthians 15:56 (NASB)

*N*ote: The Law discussed in the previous chapters gives strength to sin. We will discuss how Jesus dealt both with the law and with sin and how Paul teaches we should now look at the subject of sin (noun) and sinning (in the flesh/body).

The Sin Problem

…Jesus Christ, righteous Jesus. When he served as a sacrifice for our sins, he solved the sin problem for good—not only ours, but *the whole world's.*

1 John 2:2 (MSG)

Every priest goes to work at the altar each day, offers the same old sacrifices year in, year out, and never makes a dent in *the sin problem*. As a priest, Christ made a single sacrifice for sins, and that was it!

Hebrews 10:11 (MSG)

The *Only* Sin Left

And when he (the comforter) comes, he will convict the world of its sin, and of God's righteousness, and of the coming judgment. *The world's sin* is that it refuses to believe in me. Righteousness is available because I go to the Father, and you will see me no more.

John 16:8–10 (NLT)

If anyone hears My sayings and does *not* keep them, *I do not judge him*; for I did not come to judge the world, but to save the world. He who rejects Me and does not receive My sayings, has one who judges him; the word I spoke is *what will judge him at the last day*. For I did not speak on My own initiative, but the Father Himself who sent Me has given Me a commandment as to what to say and what to speak.

John 12:47–49 (NASB)

> There is no judgment against anyone who believes in him. *But anyone who does not believe in him* has already been judged for not believing in God's one and only Son.

> John 3:18 (NLT)

Conclusion #7

Jesus dealt with the sin problem and the sin of the whole world at his death when he said "it is finished." Jesus dealt with all sins—past, present, and future. That includes any sin any of us still has yet to commit. He was made the propitiation of *all* our sins. Because of that, the only "sin" that God holds against anyone is whether or not they believe in Christ as their savior. That is it. Once you see that, it is easier to move forward with a greater understanding of grace.

He became ...

> You know that He appeared in visible form and became Man to take away [upon Himself] sins, and in Him there is no sin [essentially and forever].

> 1 John 3:5 (AMP)

> For our sake He made Christ [virtually] to be sin who knew no sin, so that in and through Him we might become [endued with, viewed as being in, and examples of] the righteousness of God [what

we ought to be, approved and acceptable and in right relationship with Him, by His goodness].

2 Corinthians 5:21 (AMP)

Released Us from Our Sins (the Atoning Sacrifice)

Whom God displayed publicly as a propitiation in His blood through faith. This was to demonstrate His righteousness, because in the forbearance of God He passed over the sins previously committed.

Romans 3:25 (NASB)

Therefore, He had to be made like His brethren in all things, so that He might become a merciful and faithful high priest in things pertaining to God, to make propitiation for the sins of the people.

Hebrews 2:17 (NASB)

He Himself is the propitiation for our sins; and not for ours only, but also for those of the whole world.

1 John 2:2 (NASB)

In this is love: not that we loved God, but that He loved us and sent His Son to be the propitiation (the atoning sacrifice) for our sins.

1 John 4:10 (AMP)

And from Jesus Christ, the faithful witness, the firstborn of the dead, and the ruler of the kings of the earth. To Him who loves us and released us from our sins by His blood—

Revelation 1:5 (NASB)

With his own blood—not the blood of goats and calves—he entered the Most Holy Place once for all time and secured our redemption forever.

Hebrews 9:12 (NASB)

Four Questions about Confession

Consider this:

1. As believers in Christ, would we *need* to confess any sin for our salvation when Jesus was already made propitiation for that very sin?
2. Does that mean we don't believe God?
3. Do we feel the need for Christ to make another sacrifice because He didn't do it right the first time?
4. Was this verse possibly written for the unbeliever?

Mercy Seat

And in the going in of Moses unto the tent of meeting to speak with Him — he doth even hear the voice speaking unto him from off the mercy-seat which [is] upon the ark of the testimony, from between the two cherubs; and He speaketh unto him.

Numbers 7:89 (YLT)

Whom God did set forth a mercy seat, through the faith in his blood, for the shewing forth of His righteousness, because of the passing over of the bygone sins in the forbearance of God.

Romans 3:25 (YLT)

Where Jesus has entered as a forerunner for us, having become a high priest forever according to the order of Melchizedek.

Hebrews 6:20 (NASB)

So Christ has now become the High Priest over all the good things that have come. He has entered that greater, more perfect Tabernacle in heaven, which was not made by human hands and is not part of this created world. With his own blood— not the blood of goats and calves—he entered the Most Holy Place once for all time and secured our redemption forever.

Under the old system, the blood of goats and bulls and the ashes of a young cow could cleanse people's bodies from ceremonial impurity. Just think how much more the blood of Christ will purify our consciences from sinful deeds so that we can worship the living God. For by the power of the eternal Spirit, Christ offered himself to God as a perfect sacrifice for our sins. That is why he is the one who mediates a new covenant between God and people; so that all who are called can receive the eternal inheritance God has promised them. For Christ died to set them free from the penalty of the sins they had committed under that first covenant.

Hebrews 9:11–15 (NLT)

The Law Never Made Anything Perfect

For the law never made anything perfect. But now we have confidence in a better hope, through which we draw near to God.

Hebrews 7:19 (NASB)

For the Law, since it has only a shadow of the good things to come and not the very form of things, can never, by the same sacrifices which they offer continually year by year, make perfect those who draw near.

Hebrews 10:1 (NASB)

Man's Flesh Never Made Anything Perfect

Soul (Conscience) and Body (Flesh)

Corresponding to that, baptism now saves you [spirit]—not the removal of dirt from the flesh [body], but an appeal to God for a good conscience [soul]—through the resurrection of Jesus Christ,

1 Peter 3:21 (NASB)

Are you so foolish? Having begun by the Spirit, are you now being perfected by the flesh [body]?

Galatians 3:3 (NSAB)

Spirit of Man is Made 'Perfect Forever'?

For by one offering He has perfected for all time those who are sanctified.

Hebrews 10:14 (NASB)

To the company and assembly of the first-born in heaven enrolled, and to God the judge of all, and to the spirits of righteous men made perfect,

Hebrews 12:23 (NASB)

giving thanks to the Father, who has qualified us to share in the inheritance of the saints in Light. For

He rescued us from the domain of darkness, and transferred us to the kingdom of His beloved Son,

Colossians 1:12–13 (NASB)

And baptism, which is a figure [of their deliverance], does now also save you [from inward questionings and fears], not by the removing of outward body filth [bathing], but by [providing you with] the answer of a good and clear conscience (inward cleanness and peace) before God [because you are demonstrating what you believe to be yours] through the resurrection of Jesus Christ.

1 Peter 3:21 (AMP)

Having been buried with Him in baptism, in which you were also raised up with Him through faith in the working of God, who raised Him from the dead…He made you alive together with Him, having forgiven us all our transgressions, having canceled out the certificate of debt consisting of decrees against us, which was hostile to us; and He has taken it out of the way, having nailed it to the cross.

Colossians 2:12-14 (NASB)

Remember the earlier discussion about spirit, soul, and body. Our spirit is made perfect while our flesh is not. The flesh can still sin. This helps to explain how we, as spirits, can be perfect sons of God and at same time commit a sin in the flesh or even do some "good works" that do not have any consequence on our right-standing with God in Christ.

A Dead (Buried) Man (Spirit) Can't Sin

> Having been buried with Him in baptism, in which you were also raised up with Him through faith in the working of God, who raised Him from the dead. When you were dead in your transgressions and the uncircumcision of your flesh, He made you alive together with Him, having forgiven us all our transgressions, having canceled out the certificate of debt consisting of decrees against us, which was hostile to us; and He has taken it out of the way, having nailed it to the cross. When He had disarmed the rulers and authorities, He made a public display of them, having triumphed over them through Him.
>
> Colossians 2:12-15 (NASB)

Entering into this fullness is not something you figure out or achieve. It's not a matter of being circumcised or keeping a long list of laws. No, you're already in—insiders—not through some secretive initiation rite but rather through what Christ has already gone through for you, destroying the power of sin. If it's an initiation ritual you're after, you've already been through it by submitting to baptism. Going under the water was a burial of your old life; coming up out of it was a resurrection, God raising you from the dead as he did Christ. When you were stuck in your old sin-dead life, you were incapable of responding to God. God brought you alive—right along with Christ! Think of it! All sins forgiven [all means forever and ever], the slate wiped clean, that old arrest warrant canceled and nailed to Christ's cross. He stripped all the spiritual tyrants in the universe of their sham authority at the Cross and marched them naked through the streets.

Colossians 2:12-15 (MSG)

Some of the Wonderful Words Paul Uses in Colossians 2 Above.

- Buried and raised with Him
- Alive together with Him
- You're already in
- God raising you from the dead as He did Christ
- Canceled out the certificate of debt
- Taken it out of the way
- Nailed it to the cross
- Slate wiped clean
- Old arrest warrant canceled

Have a Seat Too!

I ask you again, does God give you the Holy Spirit and work miracles among you because you obey the law? Of course not! It is because you believe the message you heard about Christ.

Galatians 3:5 (NLT)

For if because of one man's trespass (lapse, offense) death reigned through that one, much more surely will those who receive [God's] overflowing grace (unmerited favor) and the free gift of righteousness [putting them into right standing with Himself] reign as kings in life through the one Man Jesus Christ (the Messiah, the Anointed One).

Romans 5:17 (AMP)

Whereas this One [Christ], after He had offered a single sacrifice for our sins [that shall avail] for all time, sat down at the right hand of God,...For by a single offering He has forever completely cleansed and perfected those who are consecrated and made holy.

Hebrews 10:12, 14 (AMP)

And raised us up with Him, and seated us with Him in the heavenly places in Christ Jesus,

Ephesians 2:6 (NASB)

What Are the Qualifications?

... Giving thanks to the Father, who has qualified us to share in the inheritance of the saints in Light.

For He rescued us from the domain of darkness, and transferred us to the kingdom of His beloved Son.

Colossians 1:12–13 (NASB)

It is not that we think we are qualified to do anything on our own. Our qualification comes from God.

2 Corinthians 3:5 (NASB)

Complete

(definition: having all parts; lacking nothing; whole; entire; full)

Now may the God of peace Himself sanctify you entirely; and may your spirit and soul and body be preserved *complete*, without blame at the coming of our Lord Jesus Christ.

1 Thessalonians 5:23 (NASB)

Finally, brethren, rejoice, be made *complete*, be comforted, be like-minded, live in peace; and the God of love and peace will be with you.

2 Corinthians 13:11 (NASB)

Now I exhort you, brethren, by the name of our Lord Jesus Christ, that you all agree and that there be no divisions among you, but that you be made *complete* in the same mind and in the same judgment.

1 Corinthians 1:10 (NASB)

And in Him you have been made *complete*, and He is the head over all rule and authority;

Colossians 2:10 (NASB)

Irreversible Blessing of Promise ... Forever

Your brother, he said, "came here falsely and took your blessing." Esau said, "Not for nothing was he named Jacob, the Heel. Twice now he's tricked me: first he took my birthright and now he's taken my blessing." He begged, "Haven't you kept back any blessing for me?" Isaac answered Esau, "I've made him your master, and all his brothers his servants, and lavished grain and wine on him. I've given it all away. What's left for you, my son?" "But don't you have just one blessing for me, Father? Oh, bless me my father! Bless me!" Esau sobbed inconsolably.

Genesis 27:35–38 (NASB)

And you, dear brothers and sisters, are children of the promise, just like Isaac. But you are now being persecuted by those who want you to keep the law, just as Ishmael, the child born by human effort, persecuted Isaac, the child born by the power of the Spirit.

But what do the Scriptures say about that? "Get rid of the slave and her son, for the son of the slave woman will not share the inheritance with the free woman's son." So, dear brothers and sisters, we are not children of the slave woman; we are children of the free woman.

Galatians 4:28–31 (NASB)

But this is the new covenant I will make … I will be their God, and they will be my people. And I will forgive their wickedness, and I will never again remember their sins…

Hebrews 8:10, 12 (NASB)

But He, having offered one sacrifice for sins for all time, SAT DOWN [remember Jesus said "it is finished"]… For by one offering He has perfected [forever] for all time those who are sanctified.

Hebrews 10:12, 14 (NASB)

EXAMPLES OF THE RICHNESS OF GOD'S GRACE

The Real Reason the People of the Synagogue Were Filled with Rage

But Gehazi, the servant of Elisha the man of God, thought, "Behold, my master has spared this Naaman the Aramean, by not receiving from his hands what he brought. As the LORD lives, I will run after him and take something from him."

2 Kings 5:20 (NASB)

And the exiles of this host of the sons of Israel, Who are among the Canaanites as far as Zarephath.

Obadiah 1:20 (NASB)

Arise, go to Zarephath, which belongs to Sidon, and stay there; behold, I have commanded a widow there to provide for you.

1 Kings 17:9 (NASB)

And He came to Nazareth, where He had been brought up; and as was His custom, He entered the synagogue on the Sabbath, and stood up to read. And the book of the prophet Isaiah was handed to Him. And He opened the book and found the place where it was written,

"THE SPIRIT OF THE Lord IS UPON ME,
BECAUSE HE ANOINTED ME TO
PREACH THE GOSPEL TO THE POOR.
HE HAS SENT ME TO PROCLAIM
RELEASE TO THE CAPTIVES,
AND RECOVERY OF SIGHT TO THE
BLIND,
TO SET FREE THOSE WHO ARE
OPPRESSED,
TO PROCLAIM THE FAVORABLE YEAR
OF THE Lord."

And He closed the book, gave it back to the attendant and sat down; and the eyes of all in the synagogue were fixed on Him. (21)And He began to say to them, "Today this Scripture has been fulfilled in your hearing." And all were speaking well of Him, and wondering at the gracious words which were falling from His lips; and they were saying, "Is this not Joseph's son?" And He said to them, "No doubt you will quote this proverb to Me, 'Physician, heal yourself! Whatever we heard was done at Capernaum, do here in your hometown as well.'" And He said, "Truly I say to you, no prophet is welcome in his hometown. But I say to you in truth, there were many widows in Israel in the days of Elijah, when the sky was shut up for three years and six months, when a great famine came over all the land; and yet Elijah was sent to none of them, but only to Zarephath, in the land of Sidon, to a woman who was a widow. And there were many lepers in Israel in the time of Elisha the prophet; and none of them was cleansed, but only Naaman the Syrian." (28) And all the people in the synagogue were filled with rage as they heard these things;

Luke 4:16–28 (NASB)

Note

All of the people in the synagogue did not get angry when Jesus said he was fulfilling scripture as the Messiah (verse 21). They were filled with rage when Jesus spoke of the grace of God for two persons (the widow and a Syrian) who were not "supposed" to be blessed since they were not part of the Abrahamic covenant nor "obedient" to the Law of Moses (verse 28).

But if it is by grace, it is no longer on the basis of works, otherwise grace is no longer grace.

Romans 11:6 (NASB)

Jesus Only Spoke of Only Two Persons Who Had Great Faith

1. The Centurion and Great Faith

And when Jesus entered Capernaum, a centurion came to Him, imploring Him, and saying, "Lord, my servant is lying paralyzed at home, fearfully tormented." Jesus *said to him, "I will come and heal him." But the centurion said, "Lord, I am not worthy for You to come under my roof, but just say the word, and my servant will be healed.

For I also am a man under authority, with soldiers under me; and I say to this one, 'Go!' and he goes, and to another, 'Come!' and he comes, and to my slave, 'Do this!' and he does it."

Now when Jesus heard this, He marveled and said to those who were following, "Truly I say to you, I have not found such great faith with anyone in Israel I say to you that many will come from east and west, and recline at the table with Abraham, Isaac and Jacob in the kingdom of heaven; but the sons of the kingdom will be cast out into the outer darkness; in that place there will be weeping and gnashing of teeth."

And Jesus said to the centurion, "Go; it shall be done for you as you have believed." And the servant was healed that very moment.

Matthew 8:5–13 (NASB)

2. A Canaanite Woman

And a Canaanite woman from that region came out and began to cry out, saying, "Have mercy on me, Lord, Son of David; my daughter is cruelly demon-possessed." But He did not answer her a word. And His disciples came and implored Him, saying, "Send her away, because she keeps shouting at us." But He answered and said, "I was sent only to the lost sheep of the house of Israel." But she came and began to bow down before Him, saying, "Lord, help me!" And He answered and said, "It is not good to take the children's bread and throw it to the dogs." But she said, "Yes, Lord; but even the dogs feed on the crumbs which fall from their masters' table." Then Jesus said to her, "O woman, your faith is great; it shall be done for you as you wish." And her daughter was healed at once.

Matthew 15:22–29 (NASB)

Question:

What two things did they have in common?

Answer:

Neither the centurion nor the Canaanite woman were under the blessing of the Abrahamic covenant..

Conclusion #8

God's grace is *only* available to *anyone* by faith. Not by works or the law, heritage, family, bloodline, wealth, status, etc.

Question:

What is unique about the women in the genealogy of Christ?

> Judah was the father of Perez and Zerah by Tamar, Perez was the father of Hezron, and Hezron the father of Ram… Salmon was the father of Boaz by Rahab, Boaz was the father of Obed by Ruth, and Obed the father of Jesse. Jesse was the father of David the king. David was the father of Solomon by Bathsheba who had been the wife of Uriah.
>
> Matthew 1:3, 5, 6 (NASB)

> Now it was about three months later that Judah was informed, " Your daughter-in-law Tamar has played the harlot, and behold, she is also with child

by harlotry." Then Judah said, "Bring her out and let her be burned!"

Genesis 38:24 (NASB)

The city shall be under the ban, it and all that is in it belongs to the LORD; only Rahab the harlot and all who are with her in the house shall live, because she hid the messengers whom we sent.

Joshua 6:17 (NASB)

They took for themselves Moabite women as wives; the name of the one was Orpah and the name of the other Ruth. And they lived there about ten years.

Ruth 1:4 (NASB)

The Law came in so that the transgression would increase; but where sin increased, grace abounded all the more,

Romans 5:20 (NASB)

Answer:

These are the only women listed in the genealogy of Christ which is determined by the male bloodline. The fact that God lists them here is an example of his grace. It's not because of anything they did except believe in God's Grace. By *religious* standards, they were out of the covenant. Again, examples that the gift of grace is not grace if it is based on works, but only by faith.

But if it is by grace, it is no longer on the basis of works, otherwise grace is no longer grace.

Romans 11:6 (NASB)

The Story of the Worst Sinner of All Time

Saul was one of the witnesses, and he agreed completely with the killing of Stephen. A great wave of persecution began that day, sweeping over the church in Jerusalem; and all the believers except the apostles were scattered through the regions of Judea and Samaria ... But Saul was going everywhere to destroy the church. He went from house to house, dragging out both men and women to throw them into prison.

Acts 8:1–3 (NLT)

Verily I say unto you, in as much as ye [Saul] have done it unto one of the least of these my brethren, ye have done it unto me.

Matthew 25:40 (NASB)

All this time Saul was breathing down the necks of the Master's disciples, out for the kill. He went to the Chief Priest and got arrest warrants to take to the meeting places in Damascus so that if he found anyone there belonging to the Way, whether men or women, he could arrest them and bring them to Jerusalem. He set off. When he got to the outskirts of Damascus, he was suddenly dazed by a blinding flash of light. As he fell to the ground, he heard [the voice of Christ]: "Saul, Saul, why are you out to get me?"

Acts 9:1–4 (MSG)

To me, PAUL, the very least of all saints, this grace was given, to preach to the Gentiles the unfathomable riches of Christ.

Ephesians 3:8 (NASB)

For I am the least of the apostles, and not fit to be called an apostle, because I persecuted the church of God.

1 Corinthians 15:9 (NASB)

For the Son of Man has come to save that which was lost.

Matthew 18:11 (NASB)

This is a trustworthy saying, and everyone should accept it: "Christ Jesus came into the world to save sinners"—and I [Paul, formerly Saul] am the worst of them all.

1 Timothy 1:15 (NLT)

COMMON QUESTIONS AND ARGUMENTS ABOUT GRACE

Here are some of the questions and arguments commonly used in understanding the scope of God's grace.

Question/Argument #1

Once we are saved, do we have to "try" to do good works in order for God to accept us and answer our prayers?

Salvation Through Christ Comes only by Faith in His Grace.

> If you confess with your mouth Jesus as Lord, and believe in your heart that God raised Him from the dead, you will be saved.
>
> Romans 10:9 (NASB)

For by grace you have been saved through faith; and that not of yourselves, it is the gift of God.

Ephesians 2:8 (NASB)

Your Righteousness and Works Are Like Filthy Rags

For we have all become like one who is unclean…, and all our righteousness (our best deeds of rightness and justice) is like filthy rags or a polluted garment; we all fade like a leaf, and our iniquities, like the wind, take us away [far from God's favor, hurrying us toward destruction].

Isaiah 64:6 (NASB)

I have seen everything in the days of my vanity (my emptiness, falsity, vainglory, and futility): there is a righteous man who perishes in his righteousness, and there is a wicked man who prolongs his life in [spite of] his evildoing.

Ecclesiastes 7:15 (NASB)

For the righteousness of God in it is revealed from faith to faith, according as it hath been written, `And the righteous one by faith shall live

Romans 1:17 (YLT)

You have been severed from Christ, you who are seeking to be justified by law; you have fallen from grace. For we through the Spirit, by faith, are waiting for the hope of righteousness. For in Christ Jesus neither circumcision nor uncircumcision means anything, but faith working through love.

Galatians 5:4 (NASB)

[Therefore, I do not treat God's gracious gift as something of minor importance and defeat its very purpose]; I do not set aside and invalidate and frustrate and nullify the grace (unmerited favor) of God. For if justification (righteousness, acquittal from guilt) comes through [observing the ritual of] the Law, then Christ (the Messiah) died groundlessly and to no purpose and in vain. [His death was then wholly superfluous.]

Galatians 2:21 (AMP)

But suppose we seek to be made right with God through faith in Christ and then we are found guilty because we have abandoned the law. Would that mean Christ has led us into sin? Absolutely not!

Galatians 2:17 (NLT)

Galatians 2:17 speaks specifically about once how we turn to Christ in faith for salvation we should not then "see ourselves as sinners." Our *spirit man* becomes perfect and righteous only through faith in Christ.

> To the general assembly and church of the firstborn who are enrolled in heaven, and to God, the Judge of all, and to the spirits of the righteous made perfect.
>
> Hebrews 12:23 (NASB)

However, our flesh (body) can still commit a sin. We are accepted in the family of God for once and for all time by faith in Christ.

Question/Argument #2

How do we address the following verse:

> For we—willfully sinning after the receiving the full knowledge of the truth — no more for sins doth there remain a sacrifice
>
> Hebrews 10:26 (YLT)

Look at verse 26 in context with the other verses in Hebrews 10 below.

> For by one offering He has perfected for all time those who are sanctified.
>
> And the Holy Spirit also testifies to us; for after saying,
>
> "THIS IS THE COVENANT THAT I WILL MAKE WITH THEM AFTER THOSE DAYS, SAYS THE LORD: I WILL PUT MY LAWS

UPON THEIR HEART, AND ON THEIR MIND I WILL WRITE THEM,"

He then says, "AND THEIR SINS AND THEIR LAWLESS DEEDS I WILL REMEMBER NO MORE."

[18] Now where there is forgiveness of these things, there is no longer any offering for sin.

Therefore, brethren, since we have confidence to enter the holy place by the blood of Jesus, by a new and living way which He inaugurated for us through the veil, that is, His flesh, and since we have a great priest over the house of God, let us draw near with a sincere heart in full assurance of faith, having our hearts sprinkled clean from an evil conscience and our bodies washed with pure water. Let us hold fast the confession of our hope without wavering, for He who promised is faithful; and let us consider how to stimulate one another to love and good deeds, not forsaking our own assembling together, as is the habit of some, but encouraging one another; and all the more as you see the day drawing near.

[26] For if we go on sinning willfully after receiving the knowledge of the truth, there no longer remains a sacrifice for sins, but a terrifying expectation of judgment and THE FURY OF A FIRE WHICH WILL CONSUME THE ADVERSARIES. Anyone who has set aside the Law of Moses dies without mercy on the testimony of two or three witnesses. How much severer punishment do you

think he will deserve who has trampled under foot the Son of God, and has regarded as unclean the blood of the covenant by which he was sanctified, and has insulted the Spirit of grace?

Hebrews 10:14–29 (NASB)

Verses 18 and 26 seem to contradict each other. They say the same thing except they speak to one who is forgiven (verse 18) and one who is not forgiven (verse 26). Doesn't the Word say that once you are saved Jesus died for your sins forever? (Hebrews 10:14). You either have forgiveness or you don't. Therefore, Hebrews 10:26 must be referring to someone who hears the Gospel and then rejects it—they "trample underfoot the Son of God."

Of how much worse punishment, do you suppose, will he be thought worthy who has trampled the Son of God underfoot, counted the blood of the covenant by which he was sanctified a common thing, and insulted the Spirit of grace?

Hebrews 10:29 (NKJV)

The world's sin is that it refuses to believe in me.

John 16:9 (NLT)

If anyone hears My sayings and does not keep them, I do not judge him; for I did not come to judge the world, but to save the world. He who rejects Me and does not receive My sayings, has one who judges him; the word I spoke is what will judge him at the last day. For I did not speak on My own initiative, but the Father Himself who sent Me has given Me a commandment as to what to say and what to speak.

John 12:47–49 (NASB)

There is no judgment against anyone who believes in him. But anyone who does not believe in him has already been judged for not believing in God's one and only Son.

John 3:18 (NLT)

In the chapter about Sin, Christ died for the sins of the whole world, once and for all. He completed the job when he said "it is finished." The only sin left is whether anyone accepts Christ or not.

And when he [the comforter] comes, he will convict the world of its sin, and of God's righteousness, and of the coming judgment. The world's sin is that it refuses to believe in me. Righteousness is available …

John 16:8-10 (NASB)

Again, please don't forget, it's not about our works, good or bad.

He calls people, but not according to their good or bad works…

Romans 9:12 (NLT)

For it is by *free* grace (God's unmerited favor) that
you are saved (delivered from judgment and made
partakers of Christ's salvation) through [your] faith.
And this [salvation] is not of yourselves [of your
own doing, it came not through your own striving],
but it is the gift of God.

Ephesians 2:8 (AMP)

Question/Argument #3

Are We to Continue in Sin
so that Grace May Increase?

*What shall we say then? Are we to continue in sin so
that grace may increase?* May it never be! How shall
we who died to sin still live in it? Or do you not
know that all of us who have been baptized into
Christ Jesus have been baptized into His death?
Therefore we have been buried with Him through
baptism into death, so that as Christ was raised
from the dead through the glory of the Father, so
we too might walk in newness of life. For if we have
become united with Him in the likeness of His
death, certainly we shall also be in the likeness of
His resurrection, knowing this, that *our old self* [your
spirit man is the real you] was crucified with Him,

in order that our body of sin might be done away with, so that we would no longer be slaves to sin; for he who has died is freed from sin.

Now if we have died with Christ, we believe that we shall also live with Him, knowing that Christ, having been raised from the dead, is never to die again; death no longer is master over Him. For the death that He died, He died to sin once for all; but the life that He lives, He lives to God. Even so *consider yourselves* [your soul] to be dead to sin, but alive to God in Christ Jesus.

Therefore do not let sin reign in *your mortal body* [flesh/body] so that you obey its lusts, and do not go on presenting the *members of your body to sin* [flesh/body] as instruments of unrighteousness; but present yourselves to God as those alive from the dead, and your members as instruments of righteousness to God. For sin shall not be master over you, for you are not under law but under grace.

What then? Shall we sin because we are not under law but under grace? May it never be! Do you not know that when you present yourselves to someone as slaves for obedience, you are slaves of the one whom you obey, either of sin resulting in death, or of obedience resulting in righteousness? But thanks be to God that though you were slaves of sin, you became obedient from the heart to that form of teaching to which you were committed, and having been freed from sin, you became slaves of righteousness. I am speaking in human terms because of the *weakness of your flesh*. For just as you presented your members as slaves to impurity and to lawlessness, resulting in further lawlessness, so now present your members as slaves to righteousness, resulting in sanctification.

For when you were slaves of sin, you were free in regard to righteousness. Therefore what benefit were you then deriving from the things of which you are now ashamed? For the outcome of those things is death. But now having been freed from sin and enslaved to God, you derive your benefit, resulting in sanctification, and the outcome, eternal life. For the wages of sin is death, but the free gift of God is eternal life in Christ Jesus our Lord.

Romans 6:1–23 (NASB)

He calls people, but not according to their good or bad works.

Romans 9:12 (NLT)

To answer this we must continue to understand that we are spirit, soul, and body. When Jesus spoke to Nicodemus about being born again, he was talking about our spirit.

Jesus answered and said to him, "Most assuredly, I say to you, unless one is born again, he cannot see the kingdom of God."

> Nicodemus said to Him, "How can a man be born when he is old? Can he enter a second time into his mother's womb and be born?"
>
> Jesus answered, "Most assuredly, I say to you, unless one is born of water and the Spirit, he cannot enter the kingdom of God. That which is born of the flesh is flesh, and that which is born of the Spirit is spirit
>
> John 3:3–6 (NKJV)

When we become born-again, our physical body doesn't change. We continue to have the same emotions and memory (soul). We can now understand that the real part of our being is our spirit. Now, we can look at our lives in that same light and understand that our body (flesh) continues to sin every day since we often let our emotions and body tell us what we should do. We can now understand that the weakness of our flesh does not nullify the work of Christ.

So what about continuing in sin? We live in a world governed by physical laws here on Earth. If we sin in our flesh we are submitting our flesh to that world, and we will suffer the consequences of that sin now in this present world. Since God is now our Father, he doesn't stop being our father when we commit a sin in our flesh.

Question: If you as a parent had a child, who robbed a bank, would you stop being their parent even though your child suffers the consequences of that sin and goes to prison?

Romans 6 is making it clear that sinning is still bad, not because it can affect our relationship with God (who made us perfect, qualified, righteous, once and for all time) but it will affect our lives on earth in a negative way. God has wisdom through direction in his Word that helps guide us into success if we would only listen and follow that direction. Even a frequent and common sin like being rude to another person can cause the relationship to be hurt or broken, but will that stop us from being a child of God?

Another great story Jesus told us about God's grace is the story of the Prodigal Son.

An Allegory: The Younger Son

And He said, "A man had two sons. The younger of them said to his father, 'Father, give me the share of the estate that falls to me.' So he divided his wealth between them. And not many days later, the younger son gathered everything together and went on a journey into a distant country, and there he squandered his estate with loose living. Now when he had spent everything, a severe famine occurred in that country and he began to be impoverished. So he went and hired himself out to one of the citizens of that country, and he sent him into his fields to feed swine. And he would have gladly filled his stomach with the pods that the swine were eating, and no one was giving anything to him. But when he came to his senses, he said, 'How many of my father's hired men have more than enough bread, but I am dying here with hunger! I will get up and go to my father, and will say to him, "Father, I have sinned against heaven, and in your sight; I am no longer worthy to be called your son; make me as one of your hired men."' So he got up and came to his father. But while he was still a long way off, his father saw him and felt compassion for him, and ran and embraced him and kissed him. And the son said to him, 'Father, I have sinned against heaven and in your sight; I am no longer worthy to be called your son.' But the father said to his slaves, 'Quickly bring out the best robe and put it on him, and put a ring on his hand and sandals on his feet; and bring the fattened calf, kill it, and let us eat and celebrate; for this son of mine was dead and has come to life again; he was lost and has been found.' And they began to celebrate.

Now his older son was in the field, and when he came and approached the house, he heard music and dancing. And he summoned one of the servants and began inquiring what these things could be. And he said to him, 'Your brother has come, and your father has killed the fattened calf because he has received him back safe and sound.' But he became angry and was not willing to go in; and his father came out and began pleading with him. But he answered and said to his father, 'Look! For so many years I have been serving you and I have never neglected a command of yours; and yet you have never given me a young

SCOTT JOHNSON

goat, so that I might celebrate with my friends; but when this son of yours came, who has devoured your wealth with prostitutes, you killed the fattened calf for him.' And he said to him, 'Son, you have always been with me, and all that is mine is yours. But we had to celebrate and rejoice, for this brother of yours was dead and has begun to live, and was lost and has been found.

Luke 15:11–32 (NASB)

The younger son lived and was blessed under grace, not by his works. His faith was in the love of his father. If he only knew how much his father really loved him he would not have had thoughts of being his servant. The older son lived and judged his relationship based on works (the law).

Three Different Translations of Romans 2:4

… Are you unmindful or actually ignorant [of the fact] that God's kindness is intended to lead you to repent (to change your mind and inner man to accept God's will)?

Romans 2:4 (AMP)

Can't you see that his kindness is intended to turn you from your sin?

Romans 2:4 (NLT)

120

Or the riches of His goodness, and forbearance, and long-suffering, dost thou despise?—not knowing that the goodness of God doth lead thee to reformation!

Romans 2:4 (YLT)

Remember, that God's goodness and grace leads people to repentance, not condemnation.

Therefore there is now no condemnation for those who are in Christ Jesus.

Romans 8:1 (NASB)

For if the ministry of condemnation has glory, much more does the ministry of righteousness abound in glory.

2 Corinthians 3:9 (NASB)

Beloved, if our heart does not condemn us, we have confidence before God.

1 John 3:21 (NASB)

So, the *Grace* of God does not give us a "license to sin" but when we least deserve it, his wonderful love for us causes us to *Want* to be obedient!

Question/Argument #4

Can we lose our salvation based on our actions? In other words, can God be an "Indian-Giver"?

If God wanted to take back our salvation for any reason, then it was never a *free gift* to begin with.

> For if because of one man's trespass (lapse, offense) death reigned through that one, much more surely will those who receive [God's] overflowing grace (unmerited favor) and the free gift of righteousness [putting them into right standing with Himself] reign as kings in life through the one Man Jesus Christ (the Messiah, the Anointed One).
>
> Romans 5:17 (AMP)

> … the free gift of God is eternal life in Christ Jesus our Lord.
>
> Romans 6:23 (NASB)

> He who did not spare His own Son, but delivered Him over for us all, how will He not also with Him freely give us all things?
>
> Romans 8:32 (NASB)

> Every good thing given and every perfect gift is from above, coming down from the Father of lights, with whom there is no variation or shifting shadow.
>
> James 1:17 (NASB)

> Now we have received, not the spirit of the world, but the Spirit who is from God, so that we may know the things freely given to us by God.

> 1 Corinthians 2:12 (NASB)

> He calls people, but not according to their good or bad works…

> Romans 9:12 (NLT)

Basically, if we believe we can "lose" our salvation by our works, aren't we saying that Adam's sin has greater force than the work of Christ and his resurrection?

Question/Argument #5

After our confession of Christ for salvation, is it necessary to repeatedly confess any sin we may commit in order for God to forgive that sin?

> Therefore leaving the elementary teaching about the Christ, let us press on to maturity, not laying again a foundation of repentance from dead works and of faith toward God

> Hebrews 6:1 (NASB)

> Every priest goes to work at the altar each day, offers the same old sacrifices year in, year out, and never makes a dent in the sin problem. As a priest, Christ made a single sacrifice for sins, and that was it!

> Hebrews 10:11 (MSG)

…Jesus Christ, righteous Jesus. When he served as a sacrifice for our sins, he solved the sin problem for good—not only ours, but the whole world's.

1 John 2:2 (MSG)

Now where there is absolute remission (forgiveness and cancellation of the penalty) of these [sins and law breaking], there is no longer any offering made to atone for sin.

Hebrews 10:18 (AMP)

Does repeated confession wash away sins when the Blood of Christ already did that?

But [that appointed time came] when Christ (the Messiah) appeared as a High Priest of the better things that have come *and* are to come. [Then] through the greater and more perfect tabernacle not made with [human] hands, that is, not a part of this material creation,

He went once for all into the [Holy of] Holies [of heaven], not by virtue of the blood of goats and calves [by which to make reconciliation between God and man], but His own blood, having found *and* secured a complete redemption (an everlasting release for us).

Hebrews 9:11–12 (AMP)

He did it once for all time, and all God wants you to do is accept his blood sacrifice by believing in your heart and confessing with your mouth, and then you will be saved, once and for all!

> That if you confess with your mouth Jesus as Lord, and believe in your heart that God raised Him from the dead, you will be saved; for with the heart a person believes, resulting in righteousness, and with the mouth he confesses, resulting in salvation.
>
> Romans 10:9–10 (NASB)

What are two of the most commonly used verses regarding confession of sins?

> If we confess our sins, He is faithful and righteous to forgive us our sins and to cleanse us from all unrighteousness.
>
> 1 John 1:9 (NASB)

> Be confessing to one another the trespasses, and be praying for one another, that ye may be healed; very strong is a working supplication of a righteous man.
>
> James 5:16 (YLT)

Or

> Confess to one another therefore your faults (your slips, your false steps, your offenses, your sins) and pray [also] for one another, that you may be healed and restored [to a spiritual tone of mind and heart]. The earnest (heartfelt, continued) prayer of a

righteous man makes tremendous power available [dynamic in its working].

James 5:16 (AMP)

Notice God never says you must confess sin for salvation. Maybe, the reason the Word talks about this is to help keep our conscience clear so we can move forward in our walk and not dwell on the past.

Brethren, I do not regard myself as having laid hold of it yet; but one thing I do: forgetting *what lies behind* and reaching forward to what lies ahead, I press on toward the goal for the prize of the upward call of God in Christ Jesus.

Philippians 3:13-15 (NASB)

Beloved, if our heart *does not condemn us*, we have confidence before God.

1 John 3:21(NASB)

When we receive grace by faith in Christ, we also receive a clear conscience. This knowledge is critical for us in our life serving God and living in confidence before God.

Wherefore, a kingdom that cannot be shaken receiving, may we have grace, through which we *may serve God* well-pleasingly, with reverence and religious fear.

Hebrews 12:28 (YLT)

There are many things God tells us to do, for example Jesus's last and only command is to "love one another." However, does our salvation depend on our obedience to this new commandment? How about all the other commands Paul tells us throughout the Gospel? There is no place recorded in the Word that says you *must* confess your sins to be saved. It only says you *must* confess that Jesus is Lord once and for all time. How can any of us continually obey everything God tells us to do? That is the whole point of the Gospel.

God's word and direction is for our success and benefit. It has been made clear through the pages of this book that our *lack of obedience* to His word does not affect our righteousness. Our righteousness is as filthy rags. Jesus took our sins, our failures, etc., so that we could have his righteousness.

> He made Him who knew no sin to be sin on our behalf, so that we might become the righteousness of God in Him.
>
> 2 Corinthians 5:17 (NASB)

> He calls people, but not according to their good or bad works…
>
> Romans 9:12 (NLT)

> And the righteous one by faith shall live.
>
> Romans 1:17 (YLT)

I have been crucified with Christ and I no longer live, but Christ lives in me. The life I now live in the body, I live by faith in the Son of God…

Galatians 2:20 (NIV)

How do we explain 1 John 1:9?

If we confess our sins, He is faithful and just to forgive us *our* sins and to cleanse us from *all* unrighteousness

1 John 1:9 (NKJV)

Does that mean we have to confess sins to be cleansed? Let's look at the beginning of 1 John to see who John was really writing to …

We proclaim to you the one who existed from the beginning, whom we have heard and seen. We saw him with our own eyes and touched him with our own hands. He is the Word of life. This one who is life itself was revealed to us, and we have seen him. And now we testify and proclaim to you that he is the one who is eternal life. He was with the Father, and then he was revealed to us. We proclaim to you what we ourselves have actually seen and heard so that you may have fellowship with us. And our fellowship is with the Father and with his Son, Jesus Christ. We are writing these things so that you may fully share our joy. This is the message we heard from Jesus and now declare to you…

1 John 1:1-5 (NLT)

John was not writing to believers, but unbelievers so that *they could share his joy,* and so that *he could have fellowship with them* by believing on Christ. Now verse 9 has meaning! An unbeliever can now know that they can be cleansed by asking Christ to forgive them.

Notice that John uses the term "all" unrighteousness. How can someone be forgiven from "all" unrighteousness (now and forever) if you have to confess sins over and over again? Then you were never forgiven from "all" of it! This also supports that this passage was written to the unbelieving Jews.

> With his own blood—not the blood of goats and calves—he entered the Most Holy Place once for all time and secured our redemption forever.
>
> Hebrews 9:12 (NASB)

Then John adds these very important points in Chapter 2.

> My dear children, I am writing this to you so that you will not sin. But if anyone does sin, we have an advocate who pleads our case before the Father. He is Jesus Christ, the one who is truly righteous. He himself is the sacrifice that atones for our sins—and not only our sins but the sins of all the world.
>
> 1 John 2:1–2 (NLT)

> I write unto you, little children, because your sins are forgiven you for his name's sake.
>
> 1 John 2:12 (KJV)

It is Jesus's blood that does the pleading for us. We don't have to confess our sins anymore. He is the propitiation of *all* of our sins *forever*. He was righteous and Jesus took our place in judgment and gave us his righteousness.

> Everyone who believes that Jesus is the Christ has become a child of God.
>
> 1 John 5:1 (NASB)

It does not say, everyone becomes a child of God "who confesses their sins" but "who believes that Jesus is the Christ."

Also, if you search all of Paul's writing, you never find him saying that you must confess your sins. That is significant and more proof that confession of specific sins is not necessary for salvation.

It is also logical and practical for this to be the truth since it is impossible for us to remember all of our sins and even know every sin we commit in the flesh.

Consider something simple and common like worry. When we worry about something we are also sinning. The Word says that "whatsoever is not of faith is sin." (Romans 14:23). Who among us confesses every time they worry about some of the smallest things? The point is simple. We cannot earn our righteousness (right standing with God) through anything we do, so we believe on what Jesus did for us, and we trade our righteousness (as filthy rags) for his righteousness (the only Holy One, the last Adam).

As a matter of fact, Paul talks to fellow believers and teaches that our body is a temple of the Holy Spirit.

> Or do you not know that your body is the temple of the Holy Spirit who is in you, whom you have from God, and you are not your own?

> 1 Corinthians 6:19 (NKJV)

This helps to prove not only that we are born-again, but that when we sin (in the flesh) we cannot corrupt our *spirit man*. Our spirit is what is saved and will live forever. Paul could have used this opportunity to teach the need to confess sins for salvation, but he never did.

Question/Argument #6

What about Ananias and Sapphira? Were they Christians when they fell dead in church?

There were at least three different men named Ananias in the book of Acts. Notice that when Paul speaks of a Christian in the Acts he uses the term—a certain disciple, and when he speaks of an unsaved person He uses the term—a certain man.

So, the Ananias who lied to the Holy Spirit was just a man, unsaved, probably religious, probably wanting to take advantage of the prosperity present in the church from all the unselfish giving. As an unsaved man, he was not under the grace of God and therefore received judgment.

But a certain man named Ananias, with Sapphira his wife, sold a possession...But Peter said, "Ananias, why has Satan filled your heart to lie to the Holy Spirit and keep back part of the price of the land for yourself?...Then Ananias, hearing these words, fell down and breathed his last. So great fear came upon all those who heard these things.

Acts 5:1, 3, 5 (NKJV)

Now there was a certain disciple at Damascus named Ananias; and to him the Lord said in a vision, "Ananias." And he said, "Here I am, Lord."...And in a vision he has seen a man named Ananias coming in and putting his hand on him, so that he might receive his sight."...Then Ananias answered, "Lord, I have heard from many about this man, how much harm he has done to Your saints in Jerusalem ... And Ananias went his way and entered the house; and laying his hands on him he said, "Brother Saul, the Lord Jesus, who appeared to you on the road as you came, has sent me that you may receive your sight and be filled with the Holy Spirit."

Acts 9:10, 12-13, 17 (NKJV)

Then a certain Ananias, a devout man according to the law, having a good testimony with all the Jews who dwelt there, ...And the high priest Ananias commanded those who stood by him to strike him on the mouth....Now after five days Ananias the high priest came down with the elders and a certain orator named Tertullus. These gave evidence to the governor against Paul.

Acts 24:1–3 (NKJV)

Question /Argument #7

Does the Holy Spirit convict Christians of sin?

However, I am telling you nothing but the truth when I say it is profitable (good, expedient, advantageous) for you that I go away. Because if I do not go away, the Comforter (Counselor, Helper, Advocate, Intercessor, Strengthener, Standby) will not come to you [into close fellowship with you]; but if I go away, I will send Him to you [to be in close fellowship with you]. And when He comes, He will convict and convince the world and bring demonstration to it about sin and about righteousness (uprightness of heart and right standing with God) and about judgment: About sin, because they do not believe in Me [trust in, rely on, and adhere to Me];

About righteousness (uprightness of heart and right standing with God), because I go to My Father, and you will see Me no longer; About judgment, because the ruler (evil genius, prince) of this world [Satan] is judged and condemned and sentence already is passed upon him.

John 16:7–11 (AMP)

Notes

The Holy Spirit does not convict the Christian of sin, but of righteousness. The only sin left is the sin of denying Christ. So, the Holy Spirit is convicting the unsaved person of that sin. (John 16)

Also notice that judgment only applies to Satan. Why? Because God already judged Jesus with the sin of the world, God doesn't judge Christians anymore since Jesus took the judgment for us. All other unsaved person will be judged on them denying Christ as their savior. (See John 12 and John 3.)

> …The world's sin is that it refuses to believe in me. Righteousness is available because I go to the Father, and you will see me no more.
>
> John 16:8–10 (NLT)

> If anyone hears My sayings and does not keep them, I do not judge him; for I did not come to judge the world, but to save the world. He who rejects Me and does not receive My sayings, has one who judges him; the word I spoke is what will judge him at the last day. For I did not speak on My own initiative, but the Father Himself who sent Me has given Me a commandment as to what to say and what to speak.
>
> John 12:47–49 (NASB)

There is no judgment against anyone who believes in him. But anyone who does not believe in him has already been judged for not believing in God's one and only Son.

John 3:18 (NLT)

Everyone who believes that Jesus is the Christ has become a child of God

1 John 5:1 (NASB)

The Benefits of the Richness of God's Grace

1. Clear/Clean Conscience

For no person will be justified (made righteous, acquitted, and judged acceptable) in His sight by observing the works prescribed by the Law. For [the real function of] the Law is to make men recognize and be conscious of sin [not mere perception, but an acquaintance with sin which works toward repentance, faith, and holy character]. But now the righteousness of God has been revealed independently and altogether apart from the Law, although actually it is attested by the Law and the Prophets, Namely, the righteousness of God which comes by believing with personal trust and confident reliance on Jesus Christ (the Messiah). [And it is meant] for all who believe. For there is no distinction,

Romans 3:20–22 (AMP)

When Gentiles who have not the [divine] Law do instinctively what the Law requires, they are a law to themselves, since they do not have the Law. They show that the essential requirements of the Law are written in their hearts and are operating there, with which their consciences (sense of right and wrong) also bear witness; and their [moral] decisions (their arguments of reason, their condemning or approving thoughts) will accuse or perhaps defend and excuse [them]

Romans 2:14-15 (AMP)

But suppose we seek to be made right with God through faith in Christ and then we are found guilty because we have abandoned the law. Would that mean Christ has led us into sin? Absolutely not!

Galatians 2:17 (NLT)

How much more surely shall the blood of Christ, Who by virtue of [His] eternal Spirit [His own preexistent divine personality] has offered Himself as an unblemished sacrifice to God, purify our consciences from dead works and lifeless observances to serve the [ever] living God?

Hebrews 9:14 (AMP)

For the Law, since it has only a shadow of the good things to come and not the very form of things, can never, by the same sacrifices which they offer continually year by year, make perfect those who draw near. Otherwise, would they not have ceased to be offered, because the worshippers, having once been cleansed, would no longer have had consciousness of sins? But in those sacrifices there is a reminder of sins year by year.

Hebrews 10:1–3 (NLT)

Now where there is absolute remission (forgiveness and cancellation of the penalty) of these [sins and law breaking], there is no longer any offering made to atone for sin

Hebrews 10:18 (AMP)

Therefore leaving the elementary teaching about the Christ, let us press on to maturity, not laying again a foundation of repentance from dead works and of faith toward God

Hebrews 6:1 (NASB)

For [as far as this world is concerned] you have died, and your [new, real] life is hidden with Christ in God.

Colossians 3:3 (AMP)

And baptism, which is a figure [of their deliverance], does now also save you [from inward questionings and fears], not by the removing of outward body filth [bathing], but by [providing you with] the answer of a good and clear conscience (inward cleanness and peace) before God [because you are demonstrating what you believe to be yours] through the resurrection of Jesus Christ.

1 Peter 3:21 (AMP)

Beloved, if our heart does not condemn us, we have confidence before God.

1 John 3:21 (NASB)

Wherefore, a kingdom that cannot be shaken receiving, may we have grace, through which we may serve God well-pleasingly, with reverence and religious fear.

Hebrews 12:28 (YLT)

2. An Abundant Life

The thief comes only in order to steal and kill and destroy. I came that they may have and enjoy life, and have it in abundance (to the full, till it overflows).

John 10:10 (AMP)

Even when we were dead (slain) by [our own] shortcomings and trespasses, He made us alive together in fellowship and in union with Christ;

[He gave us the very life of Christ Himself, the same new life with which He quickened Him, for] it is by grace (His favor and mercy which you did not deserve) that you are saved (delivered from judgment and made partakers of Christ's salvation).

Ephesians 2:5 (AMP)

3. Peace

Therefore, having been justified by faith, we have peace with God through our Lord Jesus Christ

Romans 5:1 (NASB)

Glory to God in the highest, And on earth peace among men with whom He is pleased.

Luke 2:14 (NASB)

For a brief moment I abandoned you, but with great compassion I will take you back. In a burst of anger I turned my face away for a little while. But with everlasting love I will have compassion on you," says the Lord, your Redeemer. "Just as I swore in the time of Noah that I would never again let a flood cover the earth, so now I swear that I will never again be angry and punish you.

Isaiah 54:7–9 (NLT)

4. Inheritance/Blessing of Abraham

And now I commend you to God and to the word of His grace, which is able to build you up and to give you the inheritance among all those who are sanctified.

Acts 20:32 (NASB)

What's more, the Scriptures looked forward to this time when God would declare the Gentiles to be righteous because of their faith. God proclaimed this good news to Abraham long ago when he said, "All nations will be blessed through you." So all who put their faith in Christ share the same blessing Abraham received because of his faith. But those who depend on the law to make them right with God are under his curse, for the Scriptures say, "Cursed is everyone who does not observe and obey all the commands that are written in God's Book of the Law." So it is clear that no one can be made right with God by trying to keep the law. For the Scriptures say, "It is through faith that a righteous person has life." This way of faith is very different from the way of law, which says, "It is through obeying the law that a person has life." But Christ has rescued us from the curse pronounced by the law. When he was hung on the cross, he took upon himself the curse for our wrongdoing. For it is written in the Scriptures, "Cursed is everyone who is hung on a tree."

Galatians 3:8–13 (NLT)

If you seek to be justified and declared righteous and to be given a right standing with God through the Law, you are brought to nothing and so separated (severed) from Christ. You have fallen away from grace (from God's gracious favor and unmerited blessing).

Galatians 5:4 (AMP)

For if the inheritance [of the promise depends on observing] the Law [as these false teachers would like you to believe], it no longer [depends] on the promise; however, God gave it to Abraham [as a free gift solely] by virtue of His promise... And if you belong to Christ [are in Him who is Abraham's Seed], then you are Abraham's offspring and [spiritual] heirs according to promise.

Galatians 3:18, 29 (AMP)

Therefore you are no longer outsiders (exiles, migrants, and aliens, excluded from the rights of citizens), but you now share citizenship with the saints (God's own people, consecrated and set apart for Himself); and you belong to God's [own] household

Ephesians 2:19 (AMP)

You are the descendants (sons) of the prophets and the heirs of the covenant which God made and gave to your forefathers, saying to Abraham, And in your

Seed (Heir) shall all the families of the earth be blessed and benefited.

Acts 3:25 (AMP)

Heir

Therefore you are no longer a slave but a son, and if a son, then an heir of God through Christ.

Galatians 4:7 (NKJV)

1. a person who inherits all the property of a deceased person, as by descent, relationship, will, or, legal process.
2. a person who inherits or is entitled to inherit the rank, title, position, etc., of another.

Inheritance

... giving thanks to the Father who has qualified us to be partakers of the inheritance of the saints in the light

Colossians 1:12 (nkjv)

1. something, as a quality, characteristic, or other immaterial possession received from progenitors or predecessors as if by succession: *an inheritance of family pride.*

2. portion; birthright; heritage: *Absolute rule was considered the inheritance of kings.*

5. Perfect/Complete

... giving thanks to the Father, who has qualified us to share in the inheritance of the saints in Light. For He rescued us from the domain of darkness, and transferred us to the kingdom of His beloved Son.

Colossians 1:12–13 (NASB)

It is not that we think we are qualified to do anything on our own. Our qualification comes from God.

2 Corinthians 3:5 (NLT)

For by a single offering He has forever completely cleansed and perfected those who are consecrated and made holy.

Hebrews 10:14 (AMP)

Therefore He is able also to save to the uttermost (completely, perfectly, finally, and for all time and eternity) those who come to God through Him, since He is always living to make petition to God and intercede with Him and intervene for them.

Are you so foolish? Having begun by the Spirit, are you now being perfected by the flesh?

Galatians 3:3 (NASB)

to the general assembly and church of the firstborn
who are registered in heaven, to God the Judge of
all, to the spirits of just men made perfect

Hebrews 12:23 (NKJV)

Qualified

...giving thanks to the Father who has qualified us
to share in the inheritance of the saints in light.

Colossians 1:12 (NASB)

1. having the qualities, accomplishments, etc., required
   by law or custom for getting, having, or exercising a
   right, holding an office, or the like.

Forever

Therefore He is able also to save forever those who
draw near to God through Him, since He always
lives to make intercession for them.

Hebrews 7:25 (NASB)

1. without ever ending; eternally: *to last forever.*
2. continually; incessantly; always.

Perfect

For by a single offering He has forever completely cleansed and perfected those who are consecrated and made holy.

Hebrews 10:14 (AMP)

1. conforming absolutely to the description or definition of an ideal type: *a perfect sphere.*
2. excellent or complete beyond practical or theoretical improvement: *There is no perfect legal code. The proportions of this temple are almost perfect.*
3. entirely without any flaws, defects, or shortcomings: *a perfect apple.*
4. accurate, exact, or correct in every detail: *a perfect copy.*

6. Kings and Priests

And from Jesus Christ, the faithful witness, the firstborn from the dead, and the ruler over the kings of the earth. To Him who loved us and washed us from our sins in His own blood, and has made us kings and priests to His God and Father, to Him be glory and dominion forever and ever. Amen.

Revelation 1:5–6 (NASB)

For if because of one man's trespass death reigned through that one, much more surely will those who receive [God's] overflowing grace (unmerited favor) and the free gift of righteousness [putting them into right standing with Himself] reign as kings in life through the one Man Jesus Christ.

Romans 5:17 (AMP)

7. New things

Old—Forgive in order for us to be forgiven
New—Forgive others because we have been forgiven

Behold, the former things have come to pass, Now I declare new things; Before they spring forth I proclaim them to you. You have heard; look at all this. And you, will you not declare it? I proclaim to you new things from this time, Even hidden things which you have not known.

Isaiah 42:9, 48:6 (NASB)

Therefore if anyone is in Christ, he is a new creature; the old things passed away; behold, new things have come.

2 Corinthians 5:17 (NASB)

That is what the Scriptures mean when God told him, "I have made you the father of many nations." This happened because Abraham believed in the God who brings the dead back to life and who creates new things out of nothing.

Romans 4:17 (NLT)

If the first covenant had been faultless, there would have been no need for a second covenant to replace it. But when God found fault with the people, he said: "The day is coming, says the Lord, when I will make a new covenant … This covenant will not be like the one I made with their ancestors … They did not remain faithful to my covenant … But this is the new covenant I will make … I will put my laws in their minds, and I will write them on their hearts. I will be their God, and they will be my people. And I will forgive their wickedness, and I will never again remember their sins." When God speaks of a "new" covenant, it means he has made the first one obsolete. It is now out of date and will soon disappear.

Hebrews 8:7–13 (NLT)

8. Grace Leads Everyone to God and to Repentance

Let no foul or polluting language, nor evil word nor unwholesome or worthless talk [ever] come out of your mouth, but only such [speech] as is good and beneficial to the spiritual progress of others, as is fitting to the need and the occasion, that it may be a blessing and give grace (God's favor) to those who hear it.

Ephesians 4:29 (AMP)

You husbands in the same way live with your wives in an understanding way, as with someone weaker, since she is a woman; and show her honor as a fellow heir of the grace of life, so that your prayers will not be hindered.

1 Peter 3:7 (NASB)

Or are you [so blind as to] trifle with and presume upon and despise and underestimate the wealth of His kindness and forbearance and long-suffering patience? Are you unmindful or actually ignorant [of the fact] that *God's kindness is intended to lead you to repent (to change your mind and inner man to accept God's will)?*

Romans 2:4 (AMP)

Remember, that God's goodness and grace leads people to repentance; condemnation does not.

Therefore there is now no condemnation for those who are in Christ Jesus.

Romans 8:1 (NASB)

For if the ministry of condemnation has glory, much more does the ministry of righteousness abound in glory.

2 Corinthians 3:9 (NASB)

Beloved, if our heart does not condemn us, we have confidence before God.

1 John 3:21(NASB)

9. Do You Have a Problem with a Certain Sin? How to Get Free from Sin

Do not continue offering or yielding your bodily members [and faculties] to sin as instruments (tools) of wickedness. But offer and yield yourselves to God as though you have been raised from the dead to [perpetual] life, and your bodily members [and faculties] to God, presenting them as implements of righteousness. For sin shall not [any longer] exert dominion over you, since now you are not under Law [as slaves], but under grace [as subjects of God's favor and mercy].

Romans 6:13–14 (AMP)

We are to live as though we have been raised from the dead because Jesus took our place. And the reason sin no longer has dominion over us (*anymore!*) is because we are not under the law but under grace.

Or are you [so blind as to] trifle with and presume upon and despise and underestimate the wealth of His kindness and forbearance and long-suffering patience? Are you unmindful or actually ignorant [of the fact] that God's kindness is intended to lead you to repent (to change your mind and inner man to accept God's will)?

Romans 2:4 (AMP)

For the Law, since it has only a shadow of the good things to come and not the very form of things, can never, by the same sacrifices which they offer continually year by year, make perfect those who draw near. Otherwise, would they not have ceased to be offered, because the worshipers, having once been cleansed, would no longer have had consciousness of sins? But in those sacrifices there is a reminder of sins year by year.

Hebrews 10:1–3 (NLT)

How much more surely shall the blood of Christ, Who by virtue of [His] eternal Spirit [His own preexistent divine personality] has offered Himself as an unblemished sacrifice to God, purify our consciences from dead works and lifeless observances to serve the [ever] living God?

Hebrews 9:14 (AMP)

Having a consciousness of sin makes you think about yourself. Walking under grace makes you think about the Savior. Jesus wants us to have a conscience free from sin because we will stop thinking about ourselves (our weaknesses, failures) and think about what Jesus did for us. We can be bold and unhindered to walk in that righteousness Jesus gave us to share the truth of the Gospel freely with the whole world.

Confess your righteousness in Christ, walk under his grace and begin to walk free from any sin in your life!

CONCLUSION

For through the Law comes the knowledge of sin.

Romans 3:20–21 (NASB)

Therefore when Jesus had received the sour wine, He said, "It is finished!" And He bowed His head and gave up His spirit.

John 19:30 (NASB)

With his own blood—not the blood of goats and calves—he entered the Most Holy Place once for all time and secured our redemption forever.

Hebrews 9:12 (NASB)

Jesus Christ—served as a sacrifice for our sins, he solved the sin problem for good—not only ours, but the whole worlds.

1 John 2:2 (MSG)

The world's sin is that it refuses to believe in me…

John 16:8-10 (NLT)

Free Gift

But the free gift of Christ isn't like Adam's failure. If many people died through what one person did wrong, God's grace is multiplied even more for many people with the gift—of the one person Jesus Christ—that comes through grace. The gift isn't like the consequences of one person's sin. The judgment that came from one person's sin led to punishment, but the free gift that came out of many failures led to the verdict of acquittal. If death ruled because of one person's failure, those who receive the multiplied grace and the gift of righteousness will even more certainly rule in life through the one person Jesus Christ.

Romans 5:15-17 (CEB)

Did you receive the Spirit by the works of the Law, or by hearing with faith? Are you so foolish? Having begun by the Spirit, are you now being perfected by the flesh?

Galatians 3:2–3 (AMP)

Who has saved us and called us with a holy calling, not according to our works, but according to His …

grace which was granted us in Christ Jesus from all eternity.

2 Timothy 1:9 (NASB)

He calls people, but not according to their good or bad works…

Romans 9:12 (NLT)

But if it is by grace, it is no longer on the basis of works; otherwise grace is no longer grace.

Romans 11:6 (NASB)

For the law never made anything perfect. But now we have confidence in a better hope, through which we draw near to God.

Hebrews 7:19 (NASB)

For by one offering He has perfected [forever] for all time those who are sanctified.

Hebrews 10:14 (NASB)

It is not that we think we are qualified to do anything on our own. Our qualification comes from God.

2 Corinthians 3:5 (NASB)

And in Him you have been made complete, and He is the head over all rule and authority.

Colossians 2:10 (NASB)

And raised us up with Him, and seated us with Him in the heavenly places in Christ Jesus.

Ephesians 2:6 (NASB)

But this is the new covenant I will make … I will be their God, and they will be my people. And I will forgive their wickedness, and I will never again remember their sins…

Hebrews 8:10, 12 (NASB)

He did this that He might clearly demonstrate through the ages to come the immeasurable (limitless, surpassing) riches of His free grace (His unmerited favor) in [His] kindness and goodness of heart toward us in Christ Jesus.

Ephesians 2:7 (AMP)

Do you know Christ as your savior? He has shown his grace towards you, and all you have to do is the following:

That if you confess with your mouth Jesus as Lord, and believe in your heart that God raised Him from the dead, you will be saved; for with the heart a person believes, resulting in righteousness, and with the mouth he confesses, resulting in salvation.

Romans 10:9–10 (NASB)

REVIEW FROM THE PREFACE

Reasons to study and understand the truth about God's Grace.

1. God tells us to *grow in grace.*

    You therefore, beloved, knowing this beforehand, be on your guard so that you are not carried away by the error of unprincipled men and fall from your own steadfastness, but grow in the grace and knowledge of our Lord and Savior Jesus Christ. To Him be the glory, both now and to the day of eternity. Amen.

    2 Peter 3:17-18 (NASB)

2. God tells us to be strengthened by grace.

    Do not be carried away by varied and strange teachings; for it is good for the heart to be strengthened by grace, not by foods, through which those who were so occupied were not benefited.

Hebrews 13:9 (NASB)

3. God tells us to teach the truth about grace.

> Those heretical teachers go to great lengths to flatter you, but their motives are rotten. They want to shut you out of the free world of God's grace so that you will always depend on them for approval and direction, making them feel important.

Galatians 4:17–18 (MSG)

4. Grace is meant for all people.

> For the grace of God has appeared, bringing salvation to all men.

Titus 2:11 (NASB)

5. God's grace leads people to repentance.

> Or are you (so blind as to) trifle with and presume upon and despise and underestimate the wealth of His kindness and forbearance and long-suffering patience? Are you unmindful or actually ignorant (of the fact) that God's kindness is intended to lead you to repent (to change your mind and inner man to accept God's will)?

Romans 2:4 (AMP)

6. We need God's grace in order to serve God.

Wherefore, a kingdom that cannot be shaken receiving, may we have grace, through which we may serve God well-pleasingly, with reverence and religious fear;

Hebrews 12:28 (YLT)

7. The Grace of God instructs (trains) us in godliness

For the grace of God has appeared, bringing salvation to all men, instructing us to deny ungodliness and worldly desires and to live sensibly, righteously and godly in the present age.

Titus 2:11–12 (NASB)

REFERENCE GUIDE

1. The Law and Observing the Law

- Is foolishness (Galatians 3:2–3)
- Is against the Holy Spirit (Galatians 3:2–3)
- Can't gain perfection (Galatians 3:2-3)(Hebrews 10:1–3)
- Can't earn Grace (Galatians 3:2–3)
- Can't earn promise (Romans 4:13–6)
- Law is a contract (business deal) (Romans 4:13–16, MSG)
- Ministry of death (2 Corinthians 3:5–9)
- Knowledge of sin (Romans 3:20–21)
- Severed from Christ (Galatians 5:4)
- Doesn't mean anything (Galatians 5:4)
- Slave of the law (Galatians 5:2–6, MSG)
- Cut off from Christ (Galatians 5:2–6, MSG)
- Fallen from Grace (Galatians 5:2–6, MSG)

- Frustrate Grace (Galatians 2:21)
- Nullify Grace (Galatians 2:21)
- Cannot bring a relationship with God (Galatians 5:2–6, MSG)
- Gentiles already know the it (Romans 2:14–16)
- Can never be justified (Galatians 2:16)
- Power of sin (1 Corinthians 15:56)
- God's calling is apart from it (Romans 9:12)
- Is as filthy rags (Isaiah 64:6)
- Brings death (Romans 7:8–9)
- Brings curses (Deuteronomy 27:26)

2. Results of Righteousness

- Apart from the law (Romans 3:20–22)
- Has been manifested (Romans 3:20–22)
- For all who believe (Romans 3:20–22)
- Blood released us from sins (Revelations 1:5)
- God's household (Ephesians 2:19)
- Sons of God (Galatians 4:7)
- Eyes of Lord are on them (1 Peter 3:12)
- God's gracious gift (Galatians 2:21)
- Not by law or else Christ died in vain (Galatians 2:21)
- Comes only through faith (John 1:17)
- Heirs through God (Galatians 4:7)

3. Blood of Christ and His death and Resurrection

- Destroyed the power of sin (Colossians 2:12–15)
- Released us from our sins (Revelations 1:5)
- Means no longer any offering for sin (Hebrews 10:18)
- "In vain" if righteousness can come through law (Galatians 2:21)
- Purifies our conscience (Hebrews 9:14)
- Made us righteous (Romans 5:19)
- Abolished death (2 Timothy 1:9–10)
- Propitiation (Hebrews 2:17)
- Became sin (2 Corinthians 5:21)
- Solved sin problem for good (1 John 2:2)
- Canceled the debt (Colossians 2:12-15)
- Made our spirit man perfect forever (Hebrews 12:23)
- Qualified us to share in inheritance (Colossians 1:12–13)
- Completely cleansed (Hebrews 10:14)
- For whole world (1 John 2:2)
- Single sacrifice for all time (Hebrews 10:12)

4. Grace

Defined as not based on works (Romans 11:6)
- Only by faith (Romans 4:16)

- Free (Romans 5:17)
- From Christ (Romans 5:17)
- For anyone who believes (Romans 4:16)
- To Saul (Paul) the worst sinner of all time (1 Timothy 1:15)
- No need for continual confessions (Hebrews 10:1–3)
- Gives us Holy Spirit ((Galatians 3:5)
- Gives life (John 10:10)
- Gives peace (Romans 5:1)
- Made us alive (Ephesians 2:5)
- God is no longer angry with man (Isaiah 54:9)
- Qualified us ((2 Corinthians 3:5)
- Gives us the same blessing as Abraham (Galatians 3:9)
- New Covenant (Hebrews 8:7–13)
- Appeared to all men (Titus 2:11)
- God's Household (Ephesians 2:19)

33

5 / 22

38/55